ON SCREENWRITING

ON SCREENWRITING
BY
FREDDIE GAFFNEY

auteur

First published in 2008 by
Auteur, The Old Surgery, 9 Pulford Road, Leighton Buzzard LU7 1AB
www.auteur.co.uk
Copyright © Auteur 2008

Designed by: Nikki Hamlett
Cover image: *Barton Fink* (1991) © BFI Stills
Set by AMP Ltd, Dunstable, Bedfordshire
Printed and bound in Poland; www.polskabook.co.uk

British Library Cataloguing-in-Publication Data
A catalogue record for this book is available from the British Library

ISBN (paperback): 978-1-903663-77-6
ISBN (hardback): 978-1-903663-83-7

CONTENTS

Dedication

To Laura and my children – my story.

PREFACE

Authors have been penning screenwriting books for over half a century now, full of 'insider tips' on how to make it big in Hollywood, with titles that suggest screenwriting is an art, a craft, a skill, a business, a talent, a knack, or most simply the ability to tell stories. It is, of course, all of these.

What these books seldom do is take a complete novice to the field through the steps of learning and understanding that are required to undertake any form of creative writing, be it for the Hollywood feature film, or for the college video production. That is what this book sets out to do.

It is intended that this will be a practical manual that engages with theory that can be applied to the practical constructional process. The retrospective application of theory to aid analysis (however worthy) is something for other books. Applying Propp, Todorov, Barthes, Metz *et al* to the narrative process is an activity that can inform the understanding of spectatorship, and certainly will advance the study of the mediums, but it will not necessarily lead directly to a better screenplay, or to an easier working practice. The task of this book is to proffer a set of tools that can be brought to bear to make the process more effective and the product more successfully executed.

Screenwriting is supremely undervalued in the UK, which surprises since without the screenwriter there would be no film or television, no music promos, no documentary, no nature programmes, no light entertainment. In fact, without the screenwriter the visual medium that has dominated our spare time certainly for the last 50 years if not the last century, would have withered and died. In the USA the screenwriter is lauded by the industry and given rightful credit through vastly superior payments, through position on the end credits of films / programmes, and through titles (and resulting payments) such as Executive Producer. It is not unusual to see writers receiving the same treatment as stars in the major television studios and of course Hollywood. In the UK, however, the screenwriter is often discouraged from attending a shoot, and certainly does not receive the financial rewards colleagues on the other side of the Atlantic see as their right.

This may stem from the UK education system that is definitely unsure where to place screenwriting (too 'Media' for English, too 'English' for Media), and may also be a legacy of cine-intellectuals whose ideology dictated that the focus of cinematic attention should be on the 'author' of the film, not merely on the script. However, the growth of Film and Media courses in UK schools and colleges (many offering screenwriting and production elements), and the development of successful screenwriting courses in Higher Education Institutions (either in their own right, as part of a creative writing focus, or within a production course), matched with a populist interest in film and television, have founded a new interest in writing for the screen (in all its many forms). A new sense of democracy is emerging, where anyone with a story to tell thinks 'screenplay' where they once perhaps thought 'novel', and with an increase in the opportunities for scripts to be commissioned (from short films through to television programmes for the myriad of new digital television stations), the industries are hungry for good stories.

In the UK, both the UK Film Council and Skillset (the industry's training bodies) have identified weaknesses in the screenwriting sector and have actioned funds to improve the development of screenwriters, through both education and vocationally based schemes. Television companies offer training schemes in story lining for their programmes (primarily soaps – a true training ground), and encourage those new to the screen through various new writers' schemes. Most of the Regional Film Councils offer a clear indication of their take on the problems of the film industry by focusing funding on the development of new scripts and new screenwriters, and this is echoed by the amount of development schemes funded through the European Union.

Visiting the Internet adds another dimension to the mix with countless websites offering varying degrees of advice on how to write for film and television, and numerous sites offering to critique a completed script for a small fee. Some, such as Triggerstreet.com, offer the opportunity to become active in a community of writers, each supporting and critiquing each other, and are there to aid development with the chance of producers finding and optioning the best of those scripts appearing there.

All of this indicates the growing value of the screenwriter, and yet often only serves to convince the novice that they don't know what they are doing, and have little chance of reaching the level of knowledge that will allow them to function as a professional. It is here that this book has its focus.

It has not been written as an attempt to establish an orthodoxy of approach, nor of screenplays that are deemed worthy of study. Rather I would hope that it becomes a springboard for those writers (both aspiring and experienced) who use it in experimenting with form, with character, with style and with story, and one that stimulates new writing that in turn will invigorate the mediums and develop new audiences. Aiming to foster an approach in which all stories have potential, and all mediums are valid, it is hoped that readers will engage not only with the experimentation, but also with the more traditional structures that indicate to the industry that the writer has taken the trouble to know what is expected. Whilst no executive would turn down a great idea because it was in the wrong format, there are many assistants whose sole role it is to sort the experienced from the inexperienced – and they would. I hope that this book will prevent a great idea from being missed, and again hope that those reading this book will have processes demystified, language democratised and approaches categorised, so that they will be able to rapidly gain confidence that their work is worth being seen.

As a screenwriter and teacher, my family is used to me missing birthdays, anniversaries and days at the beach as I disappear off to my office in order to write. Nevertheless, I would like to take this opportunity to thank them for their patience, consideration and support as I have worked on this book over the last year. I'd also like to thank both friends and colleagues who have helped me order my thoughts, and who have supported me in my effort to ensure this will offer real help to those compelled to write. I would like to make particular mention of John Atkinson at Auteur without whose optimism this would never have happened, and Ann Joski whose diligence has made this the book it is.

I trust you enjoy the script choices I have made, and that you see their relevance to your writing. Similarly, I anticipate that the writing activities I have designed, and both the explanations and advice I have offered, will guide and shape your writing towards success. Lastly, I hope that this work will prove a valuable companion on your journey, and that it is one that will often travel with you.

INTRODUCTION

In this chapter you will be introduced to the following:

- The reasons why screenwriting should be studied.

- The importance of underpinning knowledge of industry conventions.

- The significance of the relationship of the script to the foundation of a production.

- The importance of understanding and responding to industry standards.

Screenwriting has emerged through the twentieth century and into the twenty-first as a natural successor to the stage play and the novel, and where once a teenager's aspiration was to work in either of these two mediums they are now just as likely (if not more so) to want to write a film. Intriguingly, whilst there is a proliferation of books that offer advice on developing talents in writing the novel, and a good number that relate to play writing, there are precious few that are designed to take the aspiring screenwriter from novice, through some initial stages and eventually through to the full length screenplay – preferring instead to focus on taking them from novice to multi-million dollar Hollywood writer. There are even fewer that consider developing the aspiring writer through craft activities and writing exercises that are designed to stimulate technical ability as well as creative skills.

The essential starting point for studying screenwriting is to realise that screenwriting is *story*. Story is the essential, non-negotiable ingredient that will make or break a screenplay, and is the component that drives everything connected to the screenplay, be it action, dialogue, genre or narrative. Story is the single element without which a screenplay will not hang together, and without which it will be dysfunctional – it is, as Robert McKee describes it, the *spine*[1] of a screenplay, and without this spine the body of the work, no matter what technical support it has, will collapse.

Technique, or the craft skills of writing are useful to develop, and a technical understanding of what the mediums can offer to enable the expression of story is essential to the skilled screenwriter, but without *story* these are but the garnish on the plate without the substance of the main dish. You will have seen films and television programmes, pop promos and adverts, that were technically well executed and clearly aware of all that the medium could do, and yet were fundamentally empty and lacking substance. They left you feeling empty, despite all the devices they employed. Such works are common, particularly in industries where turnover and pace are the key demands, and where surface gloss is often mistaken for deeper meaning (the word 'postmodern' seems to be used as a 'get out' when such works are challenged).

It is a sad fact that many of these works have utilised incredible talents and an impressive array of techniques (not to mention money), all of which have been employed to cover the gnawing, nagging thought that the script itself is flawed. This, of course, is the easiest and cheapest thing to address, as it entails a lengthy line-by-line discussion with the screenwriter. Yet this is an approach that is mostly never undertaken. Once a script has gone from screenwriter to reader, has seen some re-drafting, has been taken up by a producer, adopted by director and actors, and is ready for its first slate to be taken, the repercussions of suggesting it is flawed imply that the judgements of all those so far involved are also flawed. No one would want to suggest this, and if they did, no one would want to hear it.

EXERCISE

Select a film or television programme that you have been unhappy with – it can be of any form.

Create two columns headed *Strengths*, and *Flaws*. List under *Strengths* all of the positive points about the work. List under *Flaws* all the negative things about the work.

In which column have you placed story?

Are the elements identified in *Strengths* mainly ones connected to technique?

WHY STUDY SCREENWRITING?

The study of screenwriting is often misconstrued as repackaging what is essentially a craft trade into an academic discipline, and as such many in the film and television industries, and indeed many screenwriters themselves, berate such study, often citing reasoning such as 'screenwriters are born, not made', and 'screenwriting is about feeling, not about learning'. Such attitudes are often born of having had to struggle to 'make it' in the industry, and as such believing that good writing is itself the result of such struggle. The school of hard knocks is often one that teaches to despise anyone who has taken any form of perceived shortcut and one that entrenches the attitude that a screenwriter who has studied and exercised their craft before sending scripts out to agents and producers for rejection after rejection, is somehow less worthy of the title and of any ensuing opportunities. Francis Bacon noted:

> *Crafty Men condemn Studies; Simple Men admire them; and Wise Men use them.*[2]

And it is clearly wise to build an underpinning body of knowledge about the subject that will enable the fledgling screenwriter find the confidence of structure and technique to enable their story to come to the fore and flourish.

This is not a point wasted on the bodies that represent the film and television industries in the UK with both the UK Film Council and Skillset identifying the paucity of screenwriting training in the UK, and the need to develop screenwriters as a priority in assuring the future for the UK film and television industries[3]. To this end in 2000 the UK Film Council announced The Film Training Fund with a budget of £1 million a year to support training for scriptwriters and development executives, and instituted a programme of training for writing short films. In conjunction with Skillset it has also accredited a number of degree and postgraduate screenwriting programmes across the country, and has developed the First Light Scheme designed to develop visual storytelling skills in young people through production.

These schemes, however creditable, do of course exemplify a long-standing problem with screenwriting in the UK, as they largely address the needs of many who have access to the industry already, either by virtue of class, financial status or pre-existing industry knowledge. There is still little on offer for those who want to develop themselves from having a story burning to be told, to having a completed script and the knowledge of the next steps.

Studying screenwriting will allow novice writers the opportunity to experiment, to try out styles and approaches, and to be exposed to screenwriting concepts that will make the process of storytelling in the visual medium easier, and that will result in scripts that are more likely to be read by the industries (and in turn stand more chance of being made within the industries). From concept to contract is the route that should be explored, and it is one that needs some mapping.

When approaching a story for the visual medium, a screenwriter needs to consider not only the basic cinematic or televisual nature of the story, but also whether it can be shaped (very loosely) along one of several story 'types', and whether or not it needs to be fitted into a genre (a category of film or television that has its own distinctive features by which it is identifiable).

[1] McKee, R., 1998, pp194-196

[2] Bacon, F., 1914

[3] FILM IN ENGLAND A Development Strategy for Film and the Moving Image in Screenwriting the English Regions (UK Film Council, 2000)

I. STORY

In this chapter you will be introduced to the following:

• Story types.

• Style.

• Genre.

• Themes.

• Thinking visually in a visual medium.

• Cine-literate audience.

• Moving Image key concepts for production.

Story is key to screenwriting, and the industry agrees that story is everything. However, getting the industry to agree on exactly *what* is a good story is a different matter. When Oliver Stone wrote his first draft of the film *Platoon* (1986) he met with a junior studio executive who informed him that not only was the script the worst piece of scripting he had ever read, but that the story was the worst story he had ever read too. Downhearted, but not defeated, Stone went back to the drafting process, editing and re-editing his work, sending it off to agents, producers and studios, and constantly redrafting in response to their feedback. Ten years later, he was still working on the script, but by now had come full circle back to the original draft. He had a meeting scheduled at a major Hollywood studio where he had sent this original draft. When he arrived, he was surprised to see that the junior executive who had been so critical of his script ten years earlier was not only now a senior executive at this studio, but was the senior executive who he was about to meet to discuss his script. He was even more surprised when this executive told him that *Platoon* was not only the finest script he had read in many years in Hollywood, but that the story was one of the most powerful he had come across.

So what makes a good story? Well, perhaps that is a less important question than what makes the *right* story? Part of that studio executive's initial response to Stone's script undoubtedly had little to do with either script or story quality. More pertinent would have been the connection of the subject matter to the period in which it was being proffered (or perhaps, if the executive was any good, the connection to expectations of the period in which the film would arrive in cinemas – at least two and possibly as many as four years in the future). At the time of first offering the executive would have been conscious of the American public's weariness of the Vietnam War and its growing disconnection with conflict stories. Maybe his political bias would have come into play with a Democrat desire not to glorify war, or a Republican zeal to only show the military in a positive light. Whatever the rationale, the true reason Stone's script was rejected was because it was not right for the time, for the financial backers of the time, for the audience of the time or even for the sensibilities of the time. There are many and varied reasons why a story may not be the right story – a screenwriter tries to anticipate these reasons either before commencing work on a script, or in the drafting process.

EXERCISE

Think back five years and try to think of at least five story ideas that would not have been able to be made due to their not being right (in whatever way) for the time. (Would the television script *The Trial of Tony Blair* have been commissioned five years ago, and if not, why not? Why did it recently get a commission?) List the reasons why they would not have been made.

Think of five story ideas that you would like to develop today. What obstacles stand in their way now? Can you predict any future developments (over the next two to three years) that may affect how they will be received (by financiers, producers, studios, audiences, etc.)?

Select one of these story ideas and develop strategies for overcoming the obstacles to it being received successfully (can you change the point of view from which it is told, can you revise the central characters, can you develop – or reversion – the story in a different way?).

A common difficulty that aspiring writers and students of screenwriting face is that of definitions, with story and plot often becoming interchangeable, and so it is important at this stage to define them to avoid later confusion (not only in terminology, but in practice – a story can be plotted in many ways, and a plot can be discarded easily once it is recognised that it does not affect the story).

Story is the unpicking of an event or series of events to identify the most significant elements; you could say it is the edited highlights of an event or series of events (this could be termed the narrative of the event). Often these elements are organised in chronological order, building to the point of the story (the climax, the lesson, the reason the story is worth telling).

Plot is the ordering or positioning of the elements (or narrative), the mixing up in order to create dramatic tension, to promote a viewpoint or to show authorial ingenuity. Plot is the way the story is told from opening to ending, and through all the many choices in between.

There are infinite ways of plotting a story, all of which affect the story and its meanings; none can be discarded easily. Stories can be plotted linearly or non-linearly without changing the central issue of the strength and suitability of the story itself. A story should have a raison d'être, a point, a lesson to be learned, a moral if you will, otherwise who will want to spend their valuable time listening to it? Many years ago, as a young student, I worked night shifts with a guy who would begin speaking when we came on shift at six in the evening, and still be speaking when we finished at six in the morning, and yet never came to a point to any of the tales he related. It was as if all he ever did was download information around a topic, with no ordering process, and no concept that to make it interesting it should lead to a point (hopefully one that would leave me uplifted and more knowledgeable of life, rather than leaving me wishing I'd spent the shift pushing pins in my eyes).

The novelist Mickey Spillane described the necessity of plotting a story when he wrote:

> A fiction story is like a joke. The reason you listen to a joke is to get to the punch line. Pacing a story is like sex: you start of with the teasing, then work up to the rough stuff and then all of a sudden you get the real boom-da-boom-da-boom-da-BANG, the big explosion, then you're finished. The closer to the last word you can get the climax, the better. Nobody reads a book to get to the middle, you read a book to get to the end and you hope the end is good enough to justify all the time you have spent reading it.[1]

What he identifies here is the understanding that an audience invests its time in a story and the way it is told, and (since we all know the value of time) whether this is time spent listening to family stories of long dead relatives, or time spent sitting in a darkened cinema watching the latest blockbuster, what an audience wants is a return on its investment.

STORY TYPES

Various theorists will tell you that there are only a limited number of stories in the world and that they can all be reduced down to ten, seven, five, pick a number! Whilst I find this reductive approach restrictive (particularly since it seems no more than a competition to see who can get the lowest number), there is a good lesson to be learned about originality. Screenwriters (and writers in general) regularly beat themselves up over the need for originality, often to the point of not being able to write a word for fear that they will not be original. Let's clear this up straightaway – there is no such thing as originality.

The world has been around for millions of years and humankind has been wandering around telling stories as *homo narratus* for quite a time. Those stories are based either on experience (and let's face it, in story terms, a farmer's experience of protecting the produce from the beasts of the wild is similar if they are in rural France or if they are in sub-Saharan Africa) or on imagination that is the sum of all knowledge they have been exposed to. With this in mind it is easy to state there is no originality; there is, however, significant variation on a theme, and it is this that is often mistaken for originality and allows theorists to reduce the number of stories in the world to a surprisingly small number. This small starting point should not be prohibitive (the infinite variations produced from human DNA should inspire here), as it is the variations, the plotting, the characterisation, the very combination of constructional elements that allow the writer the freedom to create.

The 'root' stories are commonly agreed to be (more or less) the following seven:

ACHILLES

This is the story of the superhuman, an individual who is almost invincible, but whose singular flaw is their downfall. Coming from the Greek legend of Achilles who was dipped in a magical river that made him impervious to weapons – however his mother held him by the heel so that part was not covered by the waters, and so became the flaw that eventually caused his death when an arrow hit his heel.

An obvious example of this is Superman, but there are plenty of others that demonstrate an Achilles story root, such as *Patton* (1970), *Downfall* (2004), and even *Catch Me If You Can* (2002).

CINDERELLA

This comes from the fairy tale where dreams do come true (with a little help along the way), despite the actions of those who want the dream for themselves. It offers a very recognisable format, with a set of hoops that need to be jumped through to achieve the goal, and a set of transformations that need to happen for success to occur (initially these were physical, but can be more sophisticated emotional or intellectual transformations).

Many teen films fall into this in some way (particularly where the outsider gets transformed into the Prom Queen, and gets the guy of her dreams, etc.) but it is also used in more mainstream movies such as *Pretty Woman* (1990) and can also be seen in 'indie' territory in films such as *Transamerica* (2005).

Transamerica

CIRCE

Coming again from Greek legend, this is the story of a sorceress who had the power of turning men into beasts. The hero Odysseus countered her magic (through the use of herbs) and after a chase forced her to restore his bewitched men to human form. It is the chase that is central to this as a story form, but more importantly a chase that ends with restoration or regeneration.

An oft-quoted example here is that of *The Blues Brothers* (1980), but other examples could include *The Italian Job* (1969) and *The Matrix* trilogy (1999–2003).

FAUST

This is another ancient tale that assumed modern form in the Renaissance period. Dr Faust is on a quest for knowledge, being consumed by his own limits, and so agrees a pact with the Devil, signed in his own blood. He gains knowledge, and through this fame and power, but, of course, when you sign away your soul to the devil, one day the debt must be paid.

Much of the work of Martin Scorsese could fall into this story form, particularly *Goodfellas* (1990), and many mainstream movies have seen Faust as a supporting framework for their plotting (such as *Wall Street* (1987) and *Apocalypse Now* (1979)).

ORPHEUS

A Greek poet and musician of legend, Orpheus descended into Hades (the land of the dead, often referred to as Hell), to retrieve his wife Eurydice, when she died. He charmed Persephone, the Queen of the Underworld, into releasing Eurydice, but then lost her again to death by ignoring the commandment not to look back at her until they were out of Hades. Central to this root story is the loss of something or someone personal, the way that loss is dealt with (and, if needs be, recovered from) and the knowledge uncovered by that loss.

The Constant Gardener (2005) could easily be seen in this mould through the very literal 'loss' in the form of a death, but films such as *Regarding Henry* (1991) – where a 'go-getting' executive 'loses' himself after a shooting, and in the process of recovery discovers another, better self – would work equally well under this root. Mainstream Hollywood fare such as *Gladiator* (2000) and *The Sixth Sense* (1999) would usefully be contextualised through this root also. More intriguing is the suggestion that both *The Full Monty* (1997) and *Munich* (2005) owe a nod of recognition in this direction.

ROMEO AND JULIET

This tale of star-crossed lovers from different sides of feuding families is obviously older than William Shakespeare's telling of it, and is certainly the one that resonates most easily with a wide range of audiences. Plucking at a central human emotion and deep desire, deep, all conquering love is pitched against violence, hatred, malice and politics, and though the result is tragedy for those involved, love wins through.

Rather obviously film versions of *Romeo and Juliet* (such as Franco Zefferelli's (1968) and Baz Luhrman's (1996)) owe their root here, but so too do films such as *Sleepless in Seattle* (1993) and *Titanic* (1997).

TRISTAN

A Celtic tale of falling in love with one who is already betrothed, whilst under the spell of a magic potion. Honour (or the light of a cleared mind) prevails and the illicit love is renounced in favour of the legitimacy of marriage. The illicit love still burns, and when dying Tristan sends for his lover, through the duplicity of his wife, she arrives too late and dies at his bedside. This story became a popular root for many medieval romances, and was recently made into a motion picture as *Tristan and Isolde* (2006).

Fatal Attraction (1987) is a film most associated with this root, but films such as *My Summer of Love* (2004) and even *Enduring Love* (2004) can be seen as rooted here.

Of course, each of these roots can combine in infinite ways with others to produce a new variant on the original story, and it is the balance between the influences of combined story types that give each film an individual flavour (or sometimes a derivative one).

ACTIVITY

Research the sources for the story types above. In some cases these stories have been carried over many thousands of years, but all of them have been with us for at least 500 years. What is it that the writers have tapped into that has made these stories identifiable as archetypes? What is it in the origins of these stories that have given them such longevity? Why do they still have the power to speak to modern audiences?

EXERCISE

Using the seven headings above, list as many films as possible that fit into a particular type. If they fit more than one type, enter them in both columns.

Which is the most popular type? Why do you think this is?

STYLE

Style, or approach, is a working tool that shapes story (either in its archetype form, or in its developed form), and the choice of style can have a dramatic affect on the way a story is perceived.

Cinderella, for example, is often delivered stylistically as a pantomime, an over-the-top comedy, where obvious villains get their comeuppance for their playing to the audience, and where the virtuous get rewarded with a few comic lines, a song and (of course) marriage to their heart's desire.

It is without doubt that Oliver Stone could have treated the story of John Kennedy's assassination in the same way in *JFK* (1991), but, of course, there would be an affect on the construction and on the reception (booing every time Lee Harvey Oswald appears on screen, shouts of 'Look behind you!' during the motorcade, and, of course, either a dramatic change in story – JFK not dying, for example – or a refocusing of the plotting to give the requisite happy ending).

Style is undoubtedly a defining factor that needs to be considered from the moment a script is conceived, but it is more than just an aesthetic concept. Rather it is central to the range of screen mediums. Currently writing for the screen can be neatly divided into two approaches: writing for cinema (the big screen) and writing for television (the small screen). Each has its distinctive style (both visually and in terms of type of story suited to it), and each bears not only its own writing conventions, but its own set of technical conventions that a writer needs to consider before deciding on where to place the story.

One of the key differences between the mediums is that of scale, the sheer size of image (and hence of event) that can be placed in front of the audience. A great example of this comes in the difference of watching *Lawrence of Arabia* (1962) at the cinema or on a television. There is a particular sequence where Omar Sharif rides out of the distant desert astride a camel, starting as a small speck on the horizon and eventually coming into close-up after several minutes of intercutting. At the cinema this is a masterpiece moment; on television the first few minutes are often cut because the image is so small that Omar Sharif does not become visible until halfway through his ride.

Similarly, television has an intimacy with its characters that leads to considerable use of close-ups and mid-shots. If this is translated to the cinema screen the width and depth available in film is wasted. Film, at its best, tends to use a lot of wide shots, with action foregrounded against an impressive landscape.

Of course, as the two mediums converge through the developments in high definition, and the size of home screens available becomes increasingly large along with the variety of viewing options (including home projection), the differences in style between the two mediums will fail to be significant (and undoubtedly at that point even the screenplay form will evolve). Where there is significant difference emerging, however, is in new mediums. Currently the moving image product available for the Internet or for mobile phones has been largely repackaged from existing film or television product. This has meant that where it has been designed for another medium it has not worked to its full potential on these new mediums. As writers increasingly interact with these new mediums, however, conventions are evolving (stylistic conventions are often merely down to repetition and convenience of production) that will mean specific approaches for these mediums will become established.

ACTIVITY

Visit BBC Television's *The Writer's Room* website (hppt://www.bbc.co.uk/ thewritersroom) and see what kinds of television they are looking for, what kinds of story, how these stories should be treated and at what length. Are they looking for product for any online, mobile or interactive services, or does it appear to be traditional in approach?

GENRE

Genre is simply another term for type or category of story and is a key component of a screenwriter's toolkit as it allows the use of a 'template' in the creation of a story. This template consists of conventions and codes that are known to the audience and allows the writer a degree of 'shorthand' or corner-cutting in constructing the story, relying on the audience to read the conventions and codes to leap the story forward without the need for much 'telling'.

Conventions are the story elements that you would expect to see in a certain type of story. In a slasher/horror movie you would expect a babysitter to probably be a pretty teenage girl, and once left alone, to probably call her boyfriend over. His role is either to disappear, or to get killed (and there are a number of established genre conventions as to how he will be killed). It is probable that the lights will go out and that the babysitter will go to the basement to work out why. Convention dictates that this is the point the chase begins that either ends in her swift dispatch (so that another girl can fight the killer and win), or in a mammoth battle ending in her despatching the killer (conventionally the killer's body will either not be found or will disappear, thereby allowing a sequel).

Codes are genre-based clues that help identify the genre, character types or actions within the story. A code can be as simple as a Stetson hat and a Winchester rifle indicating that the story is a Western, or it can have a greater significance attached to it making it an icon (a code that is symbolic of the genre). Using the slasher/horror example from above, if the babysitter goes to the kitchen for a knife, the most likely knife (and certainly the iconic knife) would be the large chef's knife. Indeed, even the absence of this icon can be a code that the audience reads – if it is not there (its absence indicated by a gap in the knife block for example, or by the babysitter actively looking for it) then the audience knows that the killer (and only the killer) must have it.

This 'shorthand' approach is one that allows the writer to move the story quickly on and also engages the audience by offering something familiar that they can take pleasure in recognising. The trick, of course, is to provide both the familiar and the different – to

EXERCISE

In the grid below, work out what you would do with the story ideas to make them work for either television or cinema. Think about what each medium does and on what scale.

Story idea	Approach for Television	Approach for Cinema
A space prison transporter crashes on a distant planet. Guards and prisoners have to fight for survival.	Some set piece special effects, but largely limited sets, few locations, close in to avoid background, possibly night scene based. Character-driven.	Big scale special effects-driven. Land/space-scapes. Focus on spectacle, size, set-piece genre plotting.
A poverty stricken girl is made homeless and has to find money for a deposit on a flat.	Some small sets, few location – small town. Running away. Is pregnant and looking for jobs. Day driven character-driven	New York. Gets job with a firm. Rich Guy falls in love with her. love story
A middle-aged man's mother dies. With his inheritance he decides to go to Spain to party.		
The government's war on drugs is going badly. It places a crack team of soldiers in the field to wipe out the drug lords.		
A pensioner, fed up of the treatment of the elderly, forms a political party and is successful enough at the elections to form a government.		
Needing to get across country for her brother's funeral, a young woman hijacks a bus.		

combine codes and conventions in a way that is fresh and that allows for a degree of unpredictability within a broadly predictable or recognisable context.

Genres are very specifically defined by their codes and conventions and it is only the repetition of these across a body of work that allows recognition of a genre. War, gangster, comedy, musical, sci-fi, horror, Westerns – these are all recognisable in their scripting through the use of conventions to tell the story, and codes that allow the audience to 'read into' the story. In a war film, when a photograph of a girlfriend is shown, the audience that is familiar with the photograph code knows that this is a likely sign of imminent death, and that convention dictates that the person showing the photograph will either be killed within seconds, or will be revealed to be dead later (probably still clutching the photograph). The screenwriter can utilise this to play with the audience and extend the genre – perhaps by delaying the death, by offering another victim to suggest

EXERCISE

Our story is one of a killer shark that is attacking swimmers off the coast of a small holiday island. As it is ruining the holiday trade, a reward is offered for its death and a number of hunters head out in pursuit.

In the grid below identify what codes and conventions you would utilise to fit the story into a particular genre.

Genre	Codes	Conventions
Romance		
Horror		
Sci-fi		
Comedy		
Musical		

the intended one is repreived, only to have them immediately die, or even by transferring the photograph (and hence the death) to someone else. The possibilities for creative scripting are actually enhanced by skilful understanding of genre, not reduced into predictable and derivative work, nor forced into parody.

Genre does not remain pure, and there are constantly evolving sub-genres (such as the horror genre dividing into monster movies, slasher movies, ghost tales, etc.) and hybrid genres (such as the sci-fi / horror or the comedy / Western). These evolutions come through the stretching, combining and reshaping of conventions and codes that screenwriters undertake to produce a new take on an old tale. Once again, story and the way it is presented are at the heart of the screenwriter's use of genre.

THEMES

A theme in a screenplay should be correctly seen as the deeper meaning underpinning the work; a deeper meaning that offers an emotional resonance allowing the audience to connect with the work and indeed, connect the disparate elements of the work.

Looking at a long running television series such as *NYPD Blue* (1993-2005) the surface story is simply about police work. Beyond that are episodic themes that simply last the duration of the particular episode and offer the audience more than the simple story, adding layers of wider meaning that allow the audience to connect the police story with their own lives — themes such as the desire for love or the consequences of betrayal. In addition to these themes, and because of the nature of the work in being a series, there are serial themes that run through the episodes (usually centering on the main characters), and offer connection and insight not only with and into the story but with and into the characters. As the series develops the audience is exposed to these same themes in successive episodes, allowing the screenwriter to write them in lightly, and to build them across the series so the audience uncovers a picture rather than being bluntly directed to the theme.

The theme is often the reason a screenwriter becomes interested in a story, and is often the thing that is the point of passion in creating the work. The difficulty with themes is that the desire to express them can lead a writer into creating unworkable plots, characters and dialogue, by placing the theme to the fore, rather than letting it emerge from the screenplay. The former approach tends to lead to a rather bluntly expressed and clunky message that is so much on the surface of the work that the rest of the screenplay appears all too obviously there to hold the theme up, and as such may appear superficial. The latter approach is one where audience members will engage with the theme on a personal level and to a personal degree, with each interpreting the theme to the level it relates to their own lives. Not only is the theme individualised, but also the audience will react individually, offering a more active and engaged response. The difficulty for many screenwriters with this approach is that it is one that hands control of meaning over to the audience, with the perceived risk that the theme will not be 'read' in the way it was intended.

Meaning is not fixed and singular, but is shifting, reactive and polysemic. A screenwriter should let go of the conceit that they have control over meaning, as any meaning is constructed by the individual audience members in response to the themes, actions, characters and dialogue presented to them in the work. A screenwriter may be able to guide an audience towards a particular response through the way the theme is articulated, but there is no guarantee that the audience will respond in the intended way (as countless screenwriters have discovered to their cost).

Similarly, theme is often not truly revealed or understood until the closing moments of the work confirm it. A screenwriter, when asked what a proposed work is 'about', will often launch into plot description rather than identify the theme that drew them to the story. A true difficulty for the screenwriter is that the end of a screenplay may not reveal the theme that drew them to the story in the first place, but instead will reveal the screenplay's own theme, something that emerges to the screenwriter as they write, and something that says much about the organic nature of constructing a screenplay.

That said, a thematic approach can be used as a tool for structuring narrative and has been since cinema matured into the form we are familiar with today. D W Griffith used a theme to connect disparate stories (ranging across millennia) in his film *Intolerance* (1916), and even identified it in the title. This is an approach that is still as valid a century later, and is evidenced in both fiction and non-fiction work. In the documentary *Koyaanisqatsi* (1982) and its partners in the trilogy, *Powaqqatsi* (1988) and *Naqoyqatsi* (2002), seemingly random images are collected together and ordered around the central theme, with the theme initially hidden in the chaotic collisions of montage, but slowly emerging and unifying the work as it progresses).

A theme can also be used structurally through repeating the central story from differing points of view, or through differing contexts. Here, the theme is the unifying concept that emerges from the repetition, and allows an audience to connect the differences to highlight the theme. *Sliding Doors* (1998) would be a useful film to consider in relation to this, as it is only through the device of parallel lives in parallel time that the deeper themes of the film can emerge and be engaged with.

Whilst the number of themes is infinite, it is sometimes useful to take a reductive approach, as with stories, in order to get clarity of view in working with them. Phil Parker recognises this when he groups them around eight thematic types: desire for justice, pursuit of love, morality of individuals, desire for order, pursuit of pleasure, fear of death, fear of the unknown and desire for validation[2].

THE DESIRE FOR JUSTICE

This is a theme that attracts many writers, and certainly underpins many 'cop' shows, courtroom dramas and (in the current trend) forensics series (*Crime Scene Investigation*, *Waking the Dead*, etc.). It can be the root of other stories such as *Bloody Sunday* ((2002) where the injustices inflicted on peace protestors are explored), and *The Mark of Cain* ((2007) where injustices meted out to Iraqi civilians by British troops come back to haunt them).

The desire for justice does not mean that the writer has to correct an injustice – sometimes it is the action arising from the desire that is the interesting focus.

THE PURSUIT OF LOVE

It is no surprise that, since this is a central component of the human condition, this is one of the most commonly utilised thematic groupings. This encompasses not only the simple romance stories (most romantic comedies, teen romances and even epic love stories, such as *Romeo and Juliet*), but also includes darker themes of obsession (in films such as *Monsieur Hire* (1989)), unhealthy passions (*Secretary* (2002)) and even murder (*Sleeping With the Enemy* (1991)).

The pursuit of love implies that it is the chase that is interesting, and whether or not love is caught is more or less important depending on the story being told. The *dénouement*, or revelation at the end of the screenplay, simply contextualises and reveals the theme on a more micro level.

THE MORALITY OF INDIVIDUALS

Choice creates conflict and conflict is at the heart of good storytelling. If a screenwriter chooses to face the characters with a moral choice of taking a virtuous path, or taking an immoral path, or of taking a path they do not choose to take, but are forced to by a sense of duty (or other motivating force), then the conflict is within the character, making the story character focused. Audiences can be presented with characters in intense emotional turmoil (*Sophie's Choice* (1982)), with comedic vice (*Fear and Loathing in Las Vegas* (1998)), with the inhumanity of humankind (*Hotel Rwanda* (2004)), with corruption at the heart of an institution (*A Few Good Men* (1992)), etc.

Under this grouping, story is less important than character in conveying the theme and the screenwriter needs to present the audience with characters that not only seem real in their actions, but also are believable in their responses to the challenges that choice presents to them.

ear and Loathing
in Las Vegas

THE DESIRE FOR ORDER

Order within an individual's life, or the ordering of society (or even of a universe), is another popular thematic grouping that resonates with audiences. Order breaking down (*Judge Dredd* (1995) or *Kramer vs. Kramer* (1979)), chaos and corruption being combated (*Batman* (1989) or *Chinatown* (1974)), order being threatened or overwhelmed (*The Lord of the Rings* trilogy (2001-03) or *Betty Blue* (1986)), or even something as simple as managing individual challenges (*Rain Man* (1989) or *Mr. Bean's Holiday* (2007)) are all encompassed by this grouping, and the theme can be expressed through plot or character-driven narratives.

The desire for order, of course, does not necessarily mean something positive and indeed it can be the root of evil. The desire for order is one of the themes that emerges out of Claude Lanzmann's epic documentary *Shoah* (1985), and as story after story is presented it becomes clear that the desire for a re-establishment of order in post - Weimar Germany, was one of the root causes of the Holocaust, yet was also one of the remedial forces after liberation. Such duality in a theme can be a source of richness for a screenwriter.

THE PURSUIT OF PLEASURE

This pursuit is again a very human drive and therefore one that tends to attract screenwriters and audiences alike. Pleasure, of course, has a cost attached to it and story here is about the weighing of cost against worth – usually pleasure is seen to be worth any cost, even self-destruction, as in *The Doors* (1991).

Comedy often uses this device as a driving force and the comedic value comes in seeing how far characters will be driven in its pursuit. In *Those Magnificent Men in Their Flying Machines* (1965) there is considerable and relentless effort to win the race (to achieve pleasure) at any cost, and this is from where the comedy emerges. Similarly, the pleasure of going home for Thanksgiving is the driving force of the comedy in *Planes, Trains & Automobiles* (1987). Nowhere is this pursuit expressed more purely than in *Ferris Beuller's Day Off* (1986) where all the comedy springs from the ingenuity of a group of teenagers intent on having a day of pleasure away from the constraints of school.

THE FEAR OF DEATH

We all know that death is an inevitable end to life, and that is why audiences and writers are attracted to this theme, as it is a true universal that transcends cultural borders. Thematically this covers a wide range of material from vampire horrors through to melodramatic weepies, but for the writer there are only two key constructional issues: how death or the threat of death is introduced, and how it is met.

In *The Sixth Sense* death pervades the film, and yet the key death comes either as a self-satisfied realisation early in the film or the intended surprise dénouement at the end. The writer presents a world where death is not an end, but where the 'person' goes on largely unseen. Similarly with *White Noise* (2005), where the dead communicate in the background hiss of tape recordings, death is actually a device for telling a story about the living.

Alternatively the focus may be on the coming to terms with loss such as in *Terms of Endearment* (1983), or *About Schmidt* (2002), where the death is a springboard, either for activity anticipating death or for activity in response to death.

FEAR OF THE UNKNOWN

This is the basis of most horror movies and a considerable slice of sci-fi also. At the heart of this is the human fear of possibility, of things not experienced and of things that challenge all that is accepted.

The key feature of most slasher horrors is the withholding of the killer's identity and the reason for their killings. Often audiences will feel dissatisfied with a story if they know the identity of the killer – it prevents them trying to apply what is within their experience to the screen events in order to make sense of them (and get satisfaction from doing so). The *raison d'être* is also withheld from audiences to intensify the fear – not knowing why something happens is torture to most people.

The X-Files television series (1993–2002) had both these techniques perfected, to the point that sometimes the 'who?' and 'why?' were not even revealed at the end of an episode in order to preserve this fear of the unknown. Even when there was a degree of revelation at the start of a story, this would often be confounded, leading both investigators and audiences back to the unknown, back to their fears.

This is not reserved solely for these two genres, however, and can often be found as a driving force in other screen stories, such as *Deliverance* (1973). It is a key starting point for many documentaries, and underpins the untangling of an existing story (the untangling of an impenetrable reality) in order either to persuade an audience that their fears are unjustified or to give them a solid basis for their fears.

THE DESIRE FOR VALIDATION

Everybody seeks a sense of worth in their lives granted by recognition of others, and so it is no surprise that this is a theme that is dealt with again and again by screenwriters, both in terms of fiction and factual writing. Most road movies, and buddy movies, have this concept at their core and it is the emotional growth of characters across the script that is the point of interest – either in their reactions to others, or in their becoming comfortable with themselves. In *Transamerica* the central character goes on both a literal and an emotional journey, seeking validation in order to honestly accept who they are, and on the way reacts to people and events that reveal the true self.

Television does not shy away from this concept either, as it underpins many of the storylines that pervade soap operas (particularly in relation to young adults as they emerge into adult roles), and is often central to great television drama. *Boys From the Blackstuff: Yozzer's Story* (1982) presents Yozzer Hughes' disintegration in the face of unemployment – a man defined and validated by his job (a similar use can be seen in *The Full Monty*). His plea of 'Go on, gis a job' was an expression of the desire for validation, and it was the lack of validation that made him all too conscious of his worthlessness to a Thatcherite Britain.

THINKING VISUALLY IN A VISUAL MEDIUM

Before writing for the visual medium, a screenwriter should move from mere spectator in order to consider the effects the tools of the medium have on the way a story is presented, and the limitations restricting the writer's craft. Poets can utilise language that their audiences would never use and novelists can present the thoughts of characters that would never otherwise be heard; but screenwriters (if they are working in mainstream production with its demand for naturalism) work solely in what can be seen, what can be heard and what can be presented as 'real'. Therefore, internal monologues tend to be banished (or become part of a generic device), emotions or intentions are expressed with words and/or actions, and poetic imagery is realised

ACTIVITY

Select a 'universal' theme from the above section (such as love, death, justice, morality, etc., - depending on the group) and ask for a show of hands to indicate who has experience of this theme in their life. As a group, explore the stories that emerge. Once the stories have been told, ask the group to consider whether they say more about events or about character.

Working in small groups, select a film or television programme that everyone is familiar with (it may help to select a genre movie here, or a single episode of a soap opera). As a group, discuss what the film or programme is about. The first responses are likely to be story based. Go round each group and challenge them to identify the key themes of their selected story, so they can get beyond the superficial supporting structure, to what it is actually about.

Individually, ask the group to consider a film or television programme they have enjoyed for whatever reason, and select a character that they particularly related to. Individuals should then be able to identify which themes the character presented to them that they connected with (these will probably be 'universals').

through *mise-en-scène* – the selected setting, how it is dressed and how it is used to present useful story elements. A character writing at his desk who becomes angry may snap a pencil tip, whilst the character wrangling with a decision may endlessly flip a coin. Emotional turmoil may be expressed by placing characters in a storm (either in terms of bad weather, or perhaps a man-made storm such as a building being blown apart), and an obsessive nature may be expressed by a catalogued and labelled wardrobe. Visual storytelling takes a new way of thinking about how to express complex non-visual concepts such as thought processes.

There are elements of visual storytelling that fall within the screenwriter's remit, and other elements that fall within that of the production team. The screenwriter needs to be immersed in the former, and conscious of the latter. All a writer has to convey the scene with is words, words that are then reinterpreted by the director, the cinematographer, the editor, the sound designer, etc. The essential thing for a screenwriter to achieve is to successfully plant a desired image or soundscape.

ACTIVITY

In a group, watch some silent comedy shorts such as those staring Harold Lloyd, Charlie Chaplin, Buster Keaton, or the Keystone Kops. Discuss how, without the use of sound they conveyed the thoughts and emotions of the characters. If they use inter-titles discuss whether the filmmaking is strong enough to convey the thoughts and emotions without inter-titles.

This is not a call for the screenwriter to fill the screenplay with technical instructions (close-up, dissolve, match cut, etc.) – quite the reverse, in fact. Put yourself in the shoes of a director whose job it is to interpret the script and put their own mark on it. Are they going to take every technical constructional instruction on board if placed in a script? Or are they more likely to think 'If I don't change this stuff, all I'm doing is putting the screenwriter's work on screen. I need to show how great I am at *my* job'? Directors, like all creatives, don't like being told what to do. It is far better to position anyone interpreting a script with an obvious option, whilst conscious that this is the one most likely they will grab onto. For example, tell a cinematographer (in the script) to track in close-up to a pair of feet and they will almost certainly find a dozen reasons why an alternative approach is better. Instead, if you present them with an obvious approach through describing the action i.e. you leave them to pick up on a good visual or aural idea and claim it as their interpretation, *Henry's feet stopped millimetres away from the tripwire. His right foot hovered momentarily before the heel rejoined its partner. Toes tapping twice decisively, his feet pivoted and moved back across the floor to the open door.*

EXERCISE

Take several pages of script from an established film or television programme (Drew's Script-o-rama is a good internet site for downloading screenplays).

Place yourself in the shoes of a director, a cinematographer, a sound designer, or an editor.

Run through the script and get a feel for the direction and motivation of the story at this point.

Read it again, this time with a view to how your chosen role will interpret it.

Write down some technical constructional notes.

Look again at the script pages and your notes. Are there places where the writer has presented you with an obvious approach that you have adopted, or any places where you have ignored the obvious in favour of another approach?

The constructional elements that fall within the role of the screenwriter include the following:

NARRATIVE FRAME

The choice of who is 'telling' which part of a story, from which point of view the narrative will be presented, is an important one as it 'frames' the story on screen. The decision of whether a scene is played out with one character on screen, or with a thousand on screen, whether it is confined to a yacht's cabin or on deck or scaled against an unending skyline, all impact on the way the storyline plays and on the subsequent decisions others will make about how to interpret the script. This even goes as far as deciding which parts of the story will be seen and which parts are left out.

LOCATION

The choice of location for where a scene is played out is not only one of dramatic intent, but also of production value. It costs far more to do night shoots than day shoots, for example, but this balances against the dramatic impact of night scenes. From a production point of view it is far better to have several scenes shot in a particular location or set (especially when it is a relatively expensive set such as the bridge of a deep space cargo vessel as in *Alien* (1979)), but from a story point of view this may not be ideal. A skilled screenwriter knows how to re-use locations in order to present a producer with an economically viable script on first reading.

This may also include elements within the location that are central to the action or symbolically inform the scene; for example, *28 Days Later...* (2002) is a story that could be set anywhere, but the screenwriter chose to begin it in London, not only for the landscape, but also for the associations the metropolis presents the audience. A London *without people* is contrary to every image commonly presented of the city, and so therefore offered a shorthand pointer to the scale of the disaster upon which the events of the film are predicated. A single figure weaving through deserted cars and debris, crossing a bridge across the Thames with Parliament and other landmarks dominating the background, is a far different image to driving over a country bridge with fields and woods surrounding it.

It is worth considering when creating a fantasy world (such as in the stories of *The Lord of the Rings*, *The Borrowers* or even cult TV show *Blake's Seven* (1978–81)) that this is a world that will eventually have to be realised on screen. Realising *anything* has a cost implication, and the more expansive and extravagant a location the more it will cost to design appropriately. You may have noticed that many of the stories from the re-launched *Dr Who* are set either on Earth in very ordinary locations, or on far distant planets or spaceships, also in very ordinary locations (that bear uncanny resemblance to locations we are more familiar with, such as mineshafts,

28 Days Later

tunnels and laboratories). The more elaborate locations are dotted across the series to give a feel of higher production values. To create a Buddhist temple complete with a thousand levitating monks is clearly a high-cost CGI moment, and the screenwriter can expect to be closely questioned on the dramatic need for such a scene.

PACE

The pace of a unit of action, of a scene and of a sequence are key to the overall feel of a finished screenplay and must be carefully structured to achieve either balance across the screenplay, or a deliberate imbalance (this, of course, runs the risk of being perceived as an error). The pace of a scene is determined firstly by the on-screen action, secondly by the number of inferred shots, and thirdly by the amount and type of dialogue. Two characters discussing life and death at a chessboard will play slower than two characters discussing life and death whilst defending the barricades amid a pitched battle. The former is likely to have fewer shots inferred, and is likely to have room for slightly longer pieces of dialogue. The latter may have exactly the same dialogue, but because of the nature of the action it is likely to be more disjointed and interrupted.

The pace and content of a scene will inform editing decisions – not only simply when to cut and the shot-to-shot transitions, but the overall editing style and rhythm of a scene. A good producer will be able to work out from the script how long it will 'sit' in post-production and therefore how much post-production will cost – this can be a commissioning deal-breaker.

DIALOGUE

Dialogue is often used poorly when writers begin a screenplay. It offers too much description, obvious exposition ('telling' of the story), clumsy expression of emotion and speech making. It is, of course, one of the key tools of characterisation (see Chapter 2) and reveals much about backstory, state of mind and intention. As a screenplay is drafted and re-drafted the dialogue tightens through editing, and eventually serves multiple functions without obviously serving a particular one.

Again, from a production point of view, scenes with dialogue present a production challenge (sound recording, Foley work, ADR work, etc.) and a cost, and it is essential that the screenwriter considers this as they prepare a scene. Without dialogue, it will be cheaper to shoot, but will it work as well, or will it work even better?

CHARACTERISATION

The physical description of a character can have an important bearing on whether a screenplay sells or not. Producers and directors can be prompted towards envisioning certain actors and actresses in a role through some judicious character description in a screenplay. Similarly, having a character express their emotions in a certain way can position the script towards or away from commercial viability (a gangster that shows rage through crushing a glass suggests actors such as Paul Newman, whereas one that shows rage by repeatedly stabbing a passer-by suggests Joe Pesci). Characterisation is not only an essential tool of storytelling (see Chapter 2), but is also an essential ingredient in the screenplay sales mix.

SOUND

Effective screenplays consider a constructed soundscape far beyond the surface layer of dialogue. The mix of atmos (the ambient sound for a particular location), spot effects (an owl hoot, a gunshot, a cash register opening), music score and even silence, is a key tool for the screenwriter, and yet is one that is often overlooked in the drive to visually tell the story.

Sound is an effective way of enabling a spectator to visualise a story. Just put a favourite CD on: do you just hear music, or do you have associative visual memories that play alongside it? The sound of breaking glass that wakens you from your sleep is not merely sound, as it also evokes the six heavily armed burglars that are downstairs plundering your living room. A screenplay should suggest to a sound designer the direction to take, and a few well-placed references to the soundscape will be invaluable, not only in getting your filmed screenplay to sound like you envisioned, but also in helping you visualise the work as you construct it.

The constructional elements that fall outside the screenwriter's domain still have the potential to be influenced with some well-placed reference points and include the following:

MISE-EN-SCÈNE

This is a French term that is often translated as 'Putting in the Scene' and for a screenwriter it is the most important element as it involves the creation of the fictional world of the screenplay. It not only includes setting, props and costume, but also (and more importantly to the 'feel' of the realisation of the script) includes colour schemes. If when writing a wartime drama you introduce the term 'muted battleship greys and khakis', you could probably expect the production designer to latch onto this and follow it through to a thematic concept. Without this term, you may find that the designer opts to present your story in glorious, vibrant Technicolor, providing a very different interpretation to the screenplay.

Similarly, a well chosen reference to particular costume elements (such as a Homburg hat), or items within a location (rather than an iron, a 'flat iron'), can clue the production design team into your thinking and will lead to a visualisation more in line with your original intent.

CINEMATOGRAPHY

It is not for the screenwriter to dictate how the screenplay should be shot, but there are approaches that can be employed to ensure a chance of having cinematographers shoot it in the way it was originally envisioned. Scale is always a key element here, and so for a more intimate framing the action should be set against more humble, everyday locations. Place the Queen in her bedroom having a conversation and the cinematography will more than likely work around mid-shots and close-ups, whereas have the same conversation in the gardens of Windsor Castle, the cinematography is likely to work around long-shots and extreme long-shots to take advantage of the landscape opportunities. Similarly, if you want two soldiers in Iraq to have an emotionally charged scene, constrain them and the scene by placing them in the front seats (or under) a Landrover (a cinematographer will automatically look to tight shot-reverse-shot here), whereas if you have them on foot patrol then the landscape around them presents visual possibilities that most cinematographers will want to exploit.

DIRECTION

Or, more specifically, directing the actors' delivery, since their portrayal of the characters you have created, and the interpretation of action and dialogue can take the finished production in directions you never envisaged. There is little wriggle-room here as this is firmly the director's territory where their vision takes over. However, again, a well-crafted screenplay provides the director with just enough dialogue and action prompts to allow their vision to be the screenwriter's vision (without them realising).

Many novice screenwriters forget that the written word takes on many interpretations when delivered, and neglect to introduce enough (but not too many) delivery instructions ('growing annoyance', 'playfully', 'screaming in defiance', etc.). Similarly, it is amazing how many lengthy conversational scenes are presented without any instructions as to a character's actions ('nervously scratches cheek', 'seductively pushes a cherry between her lips, whilst staring him hard in the eye, pauses, then spits the stone into his lap', 'heaps spoon after spoon of sugar into the coffee cup', etc.). Nature abhors a vacuum, and without these small clues as to what a director should do with an actor, a director will devise their own actions and delivery, and so will begin to move away from the original vision.

EXERCISE

Find a public place where you can observe people's interaction without drawing attention to yourself (a café, a bar, a sports meeting, etc.). For this exercise I have even used a Cathedral crypt and watched the tourists flowing through.

Thirdly, note down the facial expressions around you that capture emotions. A grimace, a smile, a raised eyebrow, blown out cheeks, etc. If you are in a tourist area (or another country), are there any facial expressions that could be ascribed to a particular national group?

Fourthly, note down any gestures that are used for visual emphasis or as idle accompaniment to conversation – the nods, shrugs, and hand waving, or the scratching, picking, and fiddling that we all do without being aware of it. It all conveys meaning. Again, are there any gestures that are particular to a national group?

Lastly – make notes on body language. Can you tell the relationship between people from the way they position themselves? Leaning in, leaning away, looking towards, looking away, arms folded, hands behind the head, etc.

THE CINE-LITERATE AUDIENCE

An advantage of writing screenplays today is that we can be confident that our audience is familiar with the form, and so is conscious of the range of devices employed to tell stories to them. This may seem like a disadvantage at first, as it surely means that the 'magic' is dispelled. I use the word 'magic' deliberately. Imagine a magician who reveals, before the trick, exactly how the trick works. A platform for disappointment? Yes, if all the magician does is exactly what was revealed to you. However, imagine how impressed you would be if, despite knowing how the trick worked, you were still surprised by the delivery, the timing and the execution of it: completely transparent and yet still with the power to affect. That is what the screenplay is.

The storytelling form has been known to its audience for millennia and the moving image has been delivering story for over a hundred years. The mechanism, the 'magic', is known to the audience, they have grown up with it; so what keeps them coming back for more? The answer is the screenwriter's advantage – familiarity with the form does not mean familiarity with the combination of elements that combine to deliver story, and it is the way a screenplay combines elements of character, dialogue, action, visual style and cinematic / televisual devices into a particular structure that can amaze and excite (and, unfortunately, disappoint and bore).

Therefore, in order to work in the visual medium it is important to have some basic understanding of the language of the medium – even if this language does not get deployed in screenplay writing. Below are a few (of many) key terms that may give you the opportunity to surprise and delight:

Bridging shot – A device used to cover a discontinuity of time or place, such as vehicle wheels turning, the dates on a calendar falling away or even an advancing arrow on a map.

Contrapuntal sound – Sound that is used in counterpoint to the image. An idyllic scene of a country village matched with the commentary from a televised boxing match should suggest that there is something amiss.

Diegetic world – The world the characters inhabit including the sights and sounds that they see and hear.

Ellipsis – The stretching or compression of screen time. A character can get on a plane at London Heathrow, and in the following scene (seconds later) can emerge from New York's La Guardia airport. Similarly, an old man can begin his dying breath, and two and a half hours later, after his entire life story has been told, his dying breath is completed.

Establishing shot – A key shot for orienting the spectator in the fictional world. Usually a wide shot at the start of a first visit to a particular location, that seldom needs repeating unless something dramatic has happened to the location across the timeframe of the screenplay.

Flashback / flashforward – A scene or sequence that takes the spectator from the diegetic present to the diegetic past, or even to the diegetic future. *CSI: Crime Scene Investigation* has introduced an exciting addition to this formula by flashing to a supposed diegetic past.

Jump cut – An in-shot cut that deliberately draws attention to itself. This is often used to display irritation at a lengthy wait, the point of view of an addict (be it drugs, drink, etc.) or the unravelling of a state of mind.

Match cut – A cut between two images that have a visual, aural or metaphorical connection, such as the turning of train wheels and the face of a clock.

Montage – At its simplest, it is the positioning of one image (with its own meaning) next to a second image (with its own meaning) to create a third meaning. Thus, image of girl (meaning: girl) placed next to image of boy (meaning: boy) may create the third meaning that they are in love. Substitute one of the images and you will find the third meaning changes. Image can also be placed against sound to create meaning (see contrapuntal sound). Where this gets really interesting is in symbolic or associative montage: start with an executive getting ready for work, looking in the mirror and gesturing a kiss towards it, then cut to his boss' bottom as the boss reverses to camera and sits at his desk. I think the association between these two shots does not need spelling out.

Narration – A voice-over linkage device used to set up, explain or conclude a screenplay. Over-used and out of fashion, it can still offer surprises. A useful comparison of its effectiveness can be made between *Blade Runner* (1982, with narration) and the re-versioned director's cut (1990, without narration).

Non-diegetic world – This is the world outside the one the screen characters experience, and is one where musical scores, intertitles (as in *Kill Bill* (2003)) and even interludes exist. This is experienced only by the spectator and not by the characters in the diegetic world. It presents some interesting opportunities, such as in *Witness* (1985) when the music playing on a car radio in the diegetic world segues into the non-diegetic world to become the musical score.

Parallel action – Where two inter-related scenes are inter-cut to suggest they are happening simultaneously. This is superbly illustrated in *The Hunt for Red October* (1990), in a sequence that cuts a Russian submarine with an American submarine, a second Russian submarine, the White House, the Kremlin, a ship in the Russian fleet, a CIA operative on a helicopter and a ship in the American fleet.

[1] Quoted by Miller, R in Cobley, P Narrative (Routledge) 2001 pg14.

[2] Parker, P, 2001, pp91-2

2. CHARACTER

In this chapter you will be introduced to the following:

• What is characterisation?

• Developing three dimensional characters.

• Motivation.

• Action.

• Character function and story.

• Character and audience.

WHAT IS CHARACTERISATION?

Characters are essential to the delivery of story, be they human characters engaged in human activities or non-human characters expressed through human traits. Without Luke Skywalker and Darth Vader, the story of *Star Wars* (1977) would be difficult to tell, and without Lady and Tramp… well, you get the picture. Story is told through character, and even in wildlife documentaries the characters express a degree of human characteristics (or have it applied by voice-over commentary) that enables audiences to engage with them.

Characterisation, however, is more than simply planting a character in a script and animating it; the creation of characters is an essential craft skill for the screenwriter. Characters bring stories to life, allowing recognisable actions and emotional connection with story, and so should be the first thought in bringing a story to script.

You should notice that story and character are intertwined and are inseparable. Good characterisation means that rather than a character being parachuted into a story, the character is built to serve a range of both story purposes and constructional purposes.

Characters should be more than simple ciphers that are only there to deliver a specific aspect of story. They should inform story and enlighten an audience to wider themes and issues that are relevant beyond the story world. Think about the story of 'The Gingerbread Man'. Each of the three principal characters (the old woman, the gingerbread man and the fox) are given mannerisms, emotions and physicality beyond that required for telling the basics of the story, and in doing so the story is enhanced. The characterisation is what has brought the story alive to successive generations and to different cultures. It is interesting to compare versions of this story to see how each culture and each generation revise the characterisations to make them relevant to their perception of the world, their needs in telling the story.

EXERCISE

Story	Possible Characters
The story of a gunslinger that terrorises a prairie town.	
The story of a cat who is brought to a new home and has to adjust to living with a dog.	
The story of a survivor of a future natural disaster.	
The story of a teacher arriving to teach unruly pupils in a rough area.	
The story of the journey of a swallow leaving a European city and heading south for the winter.	

Using the above table, think about the type of principal characters you might choose to insert to tell your story. What kind of characteristics might they exhibit? What kind of 'people' will they be? What single message will be embodied in them?

Experiment with substitute characters and characterisations. How does this substitution affect the story?

Compare your characters with those that others have decided on. Is there similarity or difference? What accounts for any similarities and differences?

Characters should come alive as you apply them to story. They are complex in the way that everyone is complex, and as alien as strangers are on a first encounter; but in the same way strangers become friends, the screenwriter should go on a journey of discovery with their characters to find out what drives them, and how they respond to situations. This may sound strange for a creative activity, but most screenwriters eventually realise that this is not so much creativity, but more discovery.

The more you discover about characters, the more you will realise that their position in relation to narrative and to story is one that will only allow them to do what their characterisation will allow them to do, and it is at the points where you contrive to get them to do the things their characterisation would not lead them to, that the narrative falls down and the story fails. If you have discovered a moral and upright citizen, then they will not suddenly become amoral and debauched, no matter what situations you throw at them. Have them discover a cheating partner – is this enough to push them against their own instincts? Have their business fail and their home repossessed – what will their reaction be: the path of honesty and hard work, or a darker path? Have their most cherished possessions taken and their loved ones slain – is this enough to redirect their characterisation? In reality (as in the script world), probably not. For this character to change direction, the alternative must already be established within them, must be part of them that is subjugated by their 'better' self.

Think about the real world for a moment. Look at the historical 'monsters' of the twentieth century. They were all ordinary people whose darker attributes surfaced as they rose to power. The situations they found themselves in encouraged the revision to their character, but the darker side would have been there irrespective of the situation. Many a biographer has made a living out of trying to find out when the darker elements first manifested themselves, but this is irrelevant, as it is the fact they are there that offers the potential for them to become prominent in reaction to a situation.

Similarly, in the real world, we have the phrase 'acting out of character' meaning doing something that you would not normally be expected to do. The diligent student who blows off an exam for a day at the funfair is acting out of character. The hardened hitman who at the last moment decides not to make the kill but instead stops to reunite a lost child with its parents would be seen as acting out of character. In both instances there is, in fact, something in their character that is just waiting for the right moment to show itself. For many, these moments never arise and other aspects of character never reveal themselves.

There are, of course, moments when the screenwriter can have their characters act out of character, but these are moments that emulate real world occasions that are affected by alcohol, drugs, mental illness, etc. Even here, however, there is often something in successful characterisation that suggests a predisposition towards these, and so allows even the out-of-character actions and behaviour to be acknowledged as within the potentiality of character.

ACTIVITY

In a group, individually take a character you are developing and let another group member assume this role. Give the other group members the barest of descriptions of them – such as 'sixteen-year-old single mum', or 'middle-aged vicar doubting his faith', or 'ageing police detective reluctantly facing retirement'.

Let the group members in role think about their attitudes and possible behaviours.

Go round the group and have each group member ask questions of those in the role of the characters that relate to attitude and action. The questions can be as varied as 'how do you do the washing up?', or 'what's your best memory?'.

Note down the responses and see how they begin to build a complex character with attitudes and behaviours of their own.

Go round the group again, this time asking questions relating to the characters' wider life and context. The questions can focus on personal relationships – 'who is your best friend?'; professional relationships – 'how well do you get on with your boss?'; or historical context – 'what is the best gig you've ever been to?'.

DEVELOPING THREE DIMENSIONAL CHARACTERS

Characters are born to inhabit a role within a story, and yet need to be so much more in order to be truly believable, truly three dimensional. In the same way that an individual is not *born* to be a soldier, an ER doctor or a traffic cop, but instead *develop* towards careers and roles, the character must have characteristics and attitudes that lead them to the job. Similarly, the character should be more than just a job, more than just a character type (or stereotype), more than just a role – in life we don't define the people we know in this way, so why should a writer do so when creating a character?

Stereotype: A fixed and widely held but oversimplified image or idea of a distinctive type of person (or thing); a person (or thing) that strongly matches such an image or idea.

Archetype: An absolutely typical example of a person (or thing); an individual that has been subsequently imitated.

The central idea in creating characters for a screenplay is to largely create archetypes, a 'typical' person that is recognisable yet not identical. Next time you are shopping in a supermarket look at the workers on the checkouts. They are a mix of genders, ages, races, builds, etc., and it is impossible to see them as one person. However, the stereotype of the checkout worker is young, female, not particularly bright and not particularly attractive. How does this compare to reality?

Not all characters need to be archetypes. There are times when stereotypes are useful. There is a widely held perception that stereotypes are negative, but of course, stereotypes present the screenwriter with the opportunity for shorthand – presenting characters and situations that are readily recognisable and (more importantly) readily predictable for the audience, allowing the screenwriter to sketch them in, in order to perform an expected function. Principal characters should rarely be stereotypes (unless there is a good reason for this), whereas minor characters (the cop that offers directions, the bank teller being robbed, the hot dog street vendor, etc.) can be usefully sketched in this way to signpost the narrative (and, of course, to save creative effort on the part of the screenwriter).

The key to understanding characters (and to understanding people, in fact) is to realise that not only do they possess externally expressed characteristics and traits, but they also possess internal aspects that influence the external. Thus, a person who is by nature a risk taker may externalise this in the way they walk, their turn of expression and even their physical characteristics. Similarly, a person who has made consistently bad relationship decisions may well be ill at ease on a date, and possibly even nervously clumsy.

When considering external traits of a character (namely the things that can be seen on screen) these are some of the aspects worth defining before setting a character loose in a screenplay:

Age, nationality/race, social class, gender, and sexual identity – These are the basics of defining a character and offer a primary building block. Some will be more important than others depending on the story context. It is very different to have a 30-year-old action hero or a 60-year-old action hero – worth comparing this age difference in *Die Hard* (1988) and the latest *Die Hard 4.0* (2007). Would it make a difference to *Hairspray* if Edna Turnblad (Divine in the original (1988), John Travolta in the musical remake (2007)) was actually played by a woman? Would the narrative (or the spectator's view of the narrative) be affected if the character of Jack Bauer in *24* was homosexual? Often a writer may make a point of creating a character in a certain way in order to demonstrate that the characteristics are not important, only to find that a producer (or worse, at a later stage, the audience) reveals that they are actually *very* important in achieving believability.

Physical characteristics – Height, build, hair, and even complexion and eye colour can be significant in defining a character. In *Fatherland* (1994) the context of the film makes these elements all the more pertinent. How a character manages their appearance, how they walk, what their mannerisms and expressions are, how they talk (and whether they use any language specific to their job or grouping – restricted code), all give vital information to define the characterisation. It is no small consideration that in *The Princess Bride* (1987) the character of Vizzini (an evil genius) is depicted as a short, balding, slight, pasty and weak man. All of this will define how the character externalises pleasure and tension – do they punch the air or smile quietly, do they brutalise others or do they merely snap a pencil?

Carry On Teacher

Ticks – You may want to give your character some physical 'ticks', unconscious mannerisms or sounds that either are a continuous feature or appear in relation to the situation. We all have these. When I am nervous I pull on my right ear lobe; a teacher friend of mine has a habit of ending his sentences in 'Okay?'; one of my old lecturers always began his lecture by coughing and adjusting his trousers, and I once observed someone at a party who would look round the room to see who was laughing before joining in. In *Carry on Teacher* (1959), and in many other similar roles, Leslie Phillips always adjusts his tie before making a pass at a woman. This becomes a visual clue to the audience of what is either about to happen (sometimes off screen or outside the narrative), or visual support to what is happening.

View of how others see them – We all have a sense of how we are seen by other people and often adjust ourselves to foster a particular view of us, and this is the same for our characters. This is explicitly expressed in the film *Alfie* (1966), where the title character spends much of his time explaining to the audience how he works to be perceived by other characters (from the very start where he is placing a folded handkerchief on his shoulder). Dramatic tension is often achieved by other characters perceiving a character in a particular way, whilst the audience is aware of their true character. Look at how knowledge of the President's true character in *Clear and Present Danger* (1994) affects the audience view of how others see him.

Dominant impression – What impact do they make when they walk into a room? What is the lasting memory of them? This is not how they would like to be seen, but how they *are* actually seen. If you think about the way the character Sam in the television series *Cheers* (1982–93) sees himself, you should then be able to compare it to how others see him.

These are all external traits that can be seen on screen. They are relatively easy to construct and should be easily visualised. More challenging both to screenwriter and to actors / directors is the visualisation of internal aspects, the views, opinions, emotions and thoughts of a character. These are more complex for the writer to construct, as ideally they need to be simply expressed, and when we think about these in ourselves they are not easy to untangle. When considering internal aspects, these are some of the things worth considering:

Dominant personality trait – Optimist or pessimist, active or passive, thinker or doer? What sums up this character's personality? The President in *Airforce One* (1997) is definitely active, a doer, whilst Miles in *Sideways* (2004) is definitely a passive pessimist.

Intelligence / knowledge – What level of intelligence does the character have? Note this is not educational level – let's face it, there are plenty of college professors who could be described as lacking intelligence (they have knowledge, however), and plenty of village idiots who have more 'common sense'. Does the character have a particular type of intelligence? Do they possess specific knowledge in relation to a job they do? Have they knowledge or skills in addition to a job they do? Gary Dove in *Sexy Beast* (2000) is not seen as having a high educational level, but he does possess both common sense and the ability to assess people. He also possesses specific skills in crime that make him 'in demand' and on which the whole story is predicated. Similarly in *Ronin* (1998) the particular knowledge and intelligence of the principal characters (especially Sam and Vincent) are unveiled across the screenplay and are used to position and manipulate audience response.

Temperament / judgement – What is their nature? Are they placid and kind, or are they quick to anger? Are they judgemental, or do they have a *laissez-faire* attitude to life? How good is their judgement? Do they take risks on people or situations, or do they take the time to make a balanced decision? Are they able to make the right move quickly or is haste an enemy to them? The quality of judgement is a factor that can be significant to the actions they perform, and to their responses to situations they find themselves in. In *The Long Kiss Goodnight* (1996), for example, Samantha Caine's ability to correctly judge a situation and act accordingly is key to the delivery of story. Indeed, it is only when she gets distracted from her 'professional' judgement (when returning to her child's room) that she comes closest to failure.

Politics / sociological traits – What is their background? Are they by nature of the left or of the right, Democrat or Republican? Do they use their class and political leanings to their advantage, or is one or both hidden for fear of prejudice? Politics and the influence of society may not be at the forefront of everyone's life, but subconsciously both will impact on the decisions and actions taken. John Carter from the television series *ER* (1994–present) is by birth of the corporate elite, of the rich and to the political right. However, in his position as ER doctor, he displays the compassionate politics of the left, hiding his wealth and birthright. These eventually come into conflict, creating some interesting storyline opportunities.

Likes / dislikes – It may be of little real consequence that a character does not like peas or cabbage, or likes to holiday in Iceland, but a limited picture of likes and dislikes will be useful in bringing them alive, and may be useful in finding ways to convey story. Our tastes often reflect deeper character traits, and so can reveal layers beyond the surface. The soldier who 'loves the smell of Napalm in the morning', the aristocrat who enjoys greasy food at the local café and the salesman who hates both the product they are selling and the people they are selling to, all have a more developed character because of their likes and dislikes. In *Raiders of the Lost Ark* (1981) Indiana Jones tells us early on that he hates snakes, and from that point on, across the franchise, he is placed in situations where he has to contend with snakes.

Interests / hobbies – Another way of deepening an understanding of character as our interests and hobbies often reflect deeper aspects of our personalities. I was rather surprised the other day when someone I have known for several years as a quiet, intellectual, reserved man, revealed in conversation that he is a microlite pilot and has already broken several microlite records. This knowledge made me look at him in a different light. Sometimes people adopt interests and hobbies because it is expected of them or their status – playing golf is often the way to improve job prospects – whilst for other people interests and hobbies are the expression of who they really are. Either way, they are central to a fuller understanding of characters, and can encourage related plot devices. In *Beverly Hills Cop II* (1987) Detective Billy Rosewood reveals his interests in guns and 'firepower', and this is seen as a character development from the first in the franchise. Similarly, when Axel Foley reveals the knack of lock picking, he implies illegal past interests/hobbies with the line 'I wasn't always a cop'.

What / who cared about – Characters do not exist in isolation and accordingly what or whom they care about is significant in defining them. A family man need not care about his family, and may prefer his work (see *Regarding Henry*) – that tells the audience something about his character. A businesswoman may not care whom she tramples over to get to the top, but may have a soft spot for the car she drives – this tells the audience something about her character. Who or what our characters would prioritise above others will define them. Look at the characters in *American Beauty* (1999); they are defined by their relationships to each other and the people or things they prioritise over those relationships.

Goals / fears – People are driven by their goals and riven by their fears, and good characterisation mirrors this. A goal can be something short term or long term, and can be of major or minor impact – to be the richest person in the world, or to remember the shopping on the way home from work. Goals drive actions and so impact on story. In *NYPD Blue* Detective Sipowicz's goal is to get through the day without a drink, and this often presents story opportunities that place him in conflict situations. Similarly fears can be short or long term and can be of major or minor impact – the film *Clockwise* (1986) revolves around the central character's fear of being late, and his readjustment in relation to his fears presents a moral to the story.

Character strengths / weaknesses / contradictions – Rounded characters have positive aspects and flaws that enable them to be perceived as recognisably real. Strengths, weaknesses and contradictions are all relative, so someone who resists torture shows a strength in the same way as someone who resists chocolate also does. Character strengths are often easier to define than weaknesses (perhaps because none of us like to admit we have weaknesses, and so find it hard to allow our characters to have them). A sophisticated use here is where the strength is also the weakness. In *The Sin Eater* (2003, aka *The Order*) Father Thomas Garrett (a secondary character) is trained to face down evil, and courageously meets the undead without backing down. However, when evil taunts him, and even his priest companion urges him to retreat, he chases evil and runs straight into a trap, his perceived character strength actually becoming his downfall.

Contradictions are yet more interesting as these present the quirky or sometimes plainly odd character features that are common in all of us, but are of interest when characters are placed against a context. There is an interesting home movie film of Adolf Hitler playing with his pet dog – why we should see this as a contradiction, I am not quite sure, but a contradiction it is; after all megalomaniac monsters are not expected to be kind to animals. Contradictions can be temporary as in *Schindler's List* (1993), where the Camp Kommondant Amon Goeth is temporarily convinced to show mercy amidst the madness of the slaughter. The contradiction is short lived as he soon returns to brutal murder as a solution to minor irritants.

Dominant impression – The sum total of all the internal aspects of characterisation is the dominant impression. This is the view that the underlying psychology of a character produces and is often the hook for an audience's perception of a character. The 'megalomaniac monster' could well be the dominant impression of a character, but does not necessarily sum up all of the aspects covered since a dominant impression does not include consideration of complexity. The character of Penny in the Channel 4 series *Teachers* (2001–present) has a very clear dominant impression, leaving her initially unlikeable, but across the episodes the complexity of her character is revealed (and the audience grows to like her).

All of this information is the micro level detail that operates and displays itself in relation to a set of more macro level contexts. We are all the sum of everything that has happened to us, and are similarly defined by who we have associated with and who we now associate with. These elements define our character growth and so should have an equal role in defining who our characters are and how they work. Among the elements that should be considered are:

Relationships – Who a character chooses to be in their life is important; but as important are the people not necessarily chosen to be in their life but who are there anyway (neighbours, employers, roommates, etc.). Primary relationships are often with lovers, family, work colleagues, but secondary relationships can be with anyone who the character comes into regular contact with. The window cleaner, the newsagent, the *maitre d'* at a favourite restaurant or even a hated parking attendant (whoever said relationships should be positive?), all are in some form of relationship with a character and these relationships will expose aspects of the characterisation. The newsagent in *Shaun of the Dead* (2004) is a minor character but their (non-) relationship with Shaun helps defines his character quickly (particularly when he scarcely notices that the newsagent has been turned into a zombie).

Culture – The culture that a character belongs to often transcends social or educational background. Club culture is a good example of this and is certainly a defining feature for characterisation. High culture tends to suggest a level of elitism, whilst low culture tends to suggest a populist agenda, but negatively it also suggests a lowest common denominator approach. The cultural context of a character may be one they have grown up in (such as being a product of a public school system) or that they have adopted (the drink culture that is prevalent in the City, for example), but either way it gives them a context to work within or to break out of. The cultural reference points of characters in *Will and Grace* (1998-2006) are used to define them (particularly the cultural snob Will Truman) and are often used as points of conflict (Will and his friend/employer Karen Walker are often in cultural conflict).

General history – The things that happen over our lives become our reference points and often define the way we speak. The term 'rationing' means more to older generations in the UK than it does to younger ones. The felling of the World Trade Center is a moment ingrained on people conscious of it at the time, and has been a reference point ever since. The events that have happened over a character's life define them and equip them with reference points that either enable or disable connection with other characters. They need not be major events, but should be of some significance – the advent of the Dyson vacuum cleaner does not rank highly on the scale of historical events, but may prove an event of significance in defining your character. The World Trade Center attack is an event that sits at the heart of the television series *CSI: NY* (2004–present), not only for its physical overshadowing of the city and its landscape but also because the lead character Mac Taylor is a widower who lost his wife in the attack.

Personal history – This is the key component to developing a character's backstory (the story outside the immediacy of the narrative). The personal history will cover schooling, family, partners, friends, successes, failures, and even events such as gigs, theatre trips, cinema visits, etc. It could usefully consider cultural history such as the evolution of taste in music, television, etc. Again, in life think of the way you categorise people by the events of their past. Thus, in *Aliens* (1986), Ripley distrusts the android Bishop due to her previous experience with a duplicitous android (Ash) whose 'special order' led to the destruction of the Nostromo and its crew. This historical event colours all of Ripley's interactions with Bishop and affects her decision making.

These ingredients, like those in a recipe, are relatively meaningless on their own. It is only when they come together that they begin to make some sense in defining a character. However, when describing a character to someone else, this level of detail is far too much and it may actually detract (particularly when talking to a producer) from 'selling' the character. The final part of building this character profile is to present something to sum up succinctly what you have built. This is done through the following:

One line descriptor – This is of use in finding a line of simple character clarity when faced with the amount of information you have put together in the character profiling you have been undertaking. John McClane (*Die Hard*) is described on the 20th Century Fox *Die Hard* website[1] as 'a barefoot cop, armed with his 9mm, his wits, and his determination'. Whilst this has the ring of marketing department copy, it does offer a pretty good summing up of McClane's character.

Everything covered so far in the examination of internal and external aspects leads to the possibility of a fully fleshed out character, one who will not necessarily do what you want, and one who will surprise you by their reactions to situations. Characterisation like this takes effort and time, but it is worth it in order to build characters that effectively write themselves.

EXERCISE

Using the Character Profile sheets below, create the principal characters for the screenplay you are working on.

Note that the first page of External Traits requires only short answers, and that the length of answer grows as you move through Internal Aspects and Contexts. Why do you think this is?

You may then want to use these to create key secondary characters. Minor subsidiary characters can be created using a cut-down version of the Character Profile, depending on what their role is.

CHARACTER PROFILE

External Traits

Age: Nationality/Race: Social Class:

Sex: Sexual Identity: Expression of Sexuality:

Physical Features:

Height: Build: Eyes:

Hair: Complexion:

Special Physical Characteristics:

Hereditary Characteristics:

Appearance:

Dress: Style: Accessories:

Grooming: Cleanliness:

Movement (including ticks):

Walking: Standing:

Facial Expressions: Gesture/Mannerisms:

Speech (including ticks):

Vocabulary: Accent: Tone:

Pitch: Pace: Rhythm:

Restricted Code:

Favourite Expressions:

Expression of Tension:

Expression of Pleasure:

View of how others perceive Image:

Dominant Impression:

INTERNAL ASPECTS

Dominant Personality Trait:

Intelligence: Knowledge:

Temperament: Quality of Judgement:

Politics: Sociological Traits:

Likes: Dislikes:

Interests: Hobbies

What/who cared about:

Goals: Fears:

Character Strengths/Weaknesses:

Contradictions:

Dominant Impression:

CONTEXT

Relationships:

Culture:

General History:

Personal History:

ONE LINE DESCRIPTOR:

MOTIVATION

Everything in storytelling should be about motivation. Deciding to take a stand against a tyrant, choosing red over black at a roulette table or getting out of bed in the morning, all are actions that should be motivated actions. But what motivates?

There are essentially two types of motivation that need to come into play when creating a screenplay:

Story motivation – Character action that is dictated by the needs of the story. If the bad guys are assembled at a warehouse across town there is little by way of conflict until we get our hero down there too. The hero's arrival is dictated by the needs of the story. Similarly, if the intention is to allow the audience to know things the character does not know, then the story-driven motivation may mean that the character has to miss some essential information (this is a standard tool in action and thriller screenplays).

Character motivation – A character's motivation may well come from the internal aspects of their character, and whilst supportive of story, this is where the screenplay becomes character-centred. Character motivation is where characters have developed a life beyond the story, and where the writer becomes more of a biographer than a creator. In *I Robot* (2004) Will Smith's character finds it hard to get out of bed. This is not necessary to the *story*, but is essential to audience understanding of his *character*.

Where screenplays become weak is where an action is not motivated, as this is where the audience questions why the character is behaving in the way they are, and this can be the point where they stop believing in the whole fictionalised world of the screenplay. This can be easily avoided by interrogating the actions of characters to assess whether they are motivated or not.

The interrogation of the screenplay is a useful device in assessing whether your characters are performing character-driven roles or whether they are there for screenwriter convenience. Quite often a screenwriter will introduce a character to fulfil a role that allows the plot to roll forward, or to deliver a set of actions they want in the screenplay for a particular reason. Interrogating the screenplay in terms of motivation of character and action will enable editing decisions such as the collapsing of multiple characters into one or the division of a character into additional characters.

ACTION

Characters inhabit a fictional world where their every action has meaning ascribed to it, and so their every action has to be considered. You will have defined so much about characterisation through the Character Profile sheets, and often screenwriters who know their characters well do not feel the need to fully articulate the actions of their characters. Familiarity may breed contempt, but in screenwriting it breeds the belief that everyone else will see what the screenwriter (who may have spent years with their characters) sees as obvious.

ACTIVITY

Ask your characters the following questions:

Who are you?

What do you want in this screenplay and why do you want it?

What are you prepared to do to get what you want, and how do you plan to get it?

Who or what is in your way, and how will you get round this?

What would stop you getting what you want?

ACTIVITY

Ask the following questions of characters' actions:

What motivated this action?

If story, how does it fit with character?

If character, what elements of character are reflected in the action?

Does the action advance the story?

Does the action advance audience understanding of the character?

Does the action reveal anything to the character about themself?

Could another character have performed the action will little or no impact on story?

Would the action be better performed by another character?

A character's action can be defined as serving two purposes, sometimes singly, sometimes in parallel: advancing story, and/or advancing understanding of character. Ideally they will do both, but at times it is expedient for them to focus more on one purpose. So, when Dr Greg Pratt in *ER* 'borrows' medial supplies to give to an unofficial church medical clinic where he also gives his time, the audience sees a side to his character that had not yet been explored. It adds a layer of depth to the character. In later episodes when someone dies due to the medicine prescribed at the clinic and Pratt is arrested, it becomes clear that this original action was not just about developing character but was actually also about progressing serial storylines.

Action is often about establishing character early in a screenplay and simultaneously setting up story elements for later in the screenplay. It is worth noting the distinction between description and action:

Description – A written or spoken account of an event, person, or object.

Action – The act or process of doing something.

One of the fundamental differences between theatre and the moving image is that the moving image deals in action, whereas theatre can happily flourish on inaction.

Description can include all the aspects of internal thought that cannot be displayed on screen (unless the often clumsy use of narration is employed), whereas action is entirely about the visual, the enactment of thought and the physical visualisation of desire. Action should be illustrative and should enable the audience to perceive something about a character – it is through our actions that people make decisions about us, and it is the same for characters.

An example of this can be seen in a central montage sequence from *The Full Monty* where the characters are seen rehearsing and carrying the rehearsals out into the rest of their lives (including the dole queue). The idea here is that rather than have them *tell* the audience that they are consumed by the idea of what they are about to do, they *show* the audience through their actions. Their actions also enable the audience to see the characters' states of mind, and their inner states, as what they do is, of course, inspired by what they feel and think (the internal aspects influencing the external aspects).

The Full Monty

The development of external actions to reflect internal aspects is one of the key skills of the screenwriter.

ACTIVITY

Complete an Action Chart (opposite) for your characters in a scene. Focus on what each of the characters are doing in each scene. Note when a character has done nothing in a scene for a while and assess whether they are needed, whether there is something they can be doing, or whether their role in the scene can be combined with another character.

EXERCISE .

Go to a busy area – a park, a tourist attraction, a shopping mall, etc. – and find a bench to sit and watch the people there.

Watch what they are doing and how their actions reflect their moods. Notice an angry parent dragging a child along, the bored teenager who does not want to be there, the busy worker dashing out to shop in a break. How do they manifest their emotions? What are their actions?

Note down some descriptions of actions that you have observed. Try to capture the mood of what is going on using adverbs (angrily, emphatically, happily, etc.).

ACTION CHART

Scene No	Type of Scene	Scene Description	Central Character	Character 1	Character 2	Character 3	Character 4
Example scene 33	Action	Harry goes to the warehouse with Terri and uncovers a plot	Harry to discover the villains' plot	Terri to save Harry's life	Mr Montego to be seen in the warehouse, revealing his role	Hatcher to attack Harry and escape with the bomb	Henchman to get killed by Terri

CHARACTER FUNCTION AND STORY

Characters are placed in a story in order to illustrate the story and express its themes and messages. They are also there as structural devices that enable the story to be expressed in a certain way. Both of these concepts that underpin the development of character present difficulties to any screenwriter engaged either in factual storytelling or the creation of fictional drama based on actual events, as they often feel the pressure of real characters whose role in actual events have significance, but may be fundamentally undramatic.

The actions of real world characters can often be expressed better though attributing their actions and function to another character. The creation of 'hybrid' characters is a decision based either on structural issues, or on the need to create drama. The key to the creation of characters is to understand what function they have in the story, and what demands are made on the character's actions by their function.

Protagonist – The protagonist is essentially our 'hero' and is the central character in the story – often the story is the story of the protagonist. The protagonist always has much to lose, and so is constantly active in driving the story forward to achieve their goals. They effectively 'carry' the story and when they achieve their goal, or (more unlikely, but possible) if they fail to achieve their goal, then the story reaches an end. In terms of screen time, the protagonist will occupy the majority of scenes.

For the protagonist to move the story forward, they must face obstacles that force them to choose a new direction or to struggle to overcome the obstacle and in doing so discover something about themselves. Facing these obstacles forces the character to change and grow, and this is often illustrative of the themes of the story.

In the French feature film *Jean de Florette* (1986), Jean arrives at the village with a plan to farm the land, but to do so requires water. When his spring dries (due to the unscrupulous actions of locals) he and his family are forced to carry water from another spring some distance away. Seeing the distress on his family and the ineffectuality of the action provokes him to begin digging a well. The backbreaking work takes its toll, leading him to use dynamite, which in turn leads to his eventual death. Obstacles provoke action, and action moves the protagonist and the story forward.

Adjuster – This character's function is to help adjust or modify the direction or actions of the protagonist. Hollywood often has a woman introduced as the adjuster (as in *Dave* (1993)), whereas television drama usually utilises the *sidekick* to act as adjuster (as in *Inspector Morse* (1987–2000)). The results of the adjuster's actions are change and growth in the protagonist's character and so they have a pivotal role in the illustration of themes and messages, and in advancing the story. Unlike the protagonist, the adjuster is likely to be at the same place at the end of the story as they were at the beginning – they undergo no significant change or growth of their own (if they did, this would decrease focus on the protagonist's change and growth).

Antagonist – The character that is in principal opposition to the protagonist and whose actions place obstacles in the way of the protagonist. There may be a number of oppositional characters in a story, but the antagonist is key in relation to the protagonist, as they are the catalyst for the actions of the protagonist and hence the events of the story. In *The Bourne Identity* (2002) Jason Bourne is faced with countless adversaries, but they are all directed by the antagonist, his ex-boss Ward Abbott.

An antagonist does not necessarily have to be human (or in vaguely humanoid form) and can be an institution or even a force. In *The Day After Tomorrow* (2004), it is global warming that assumes the key antagonist role, with nature and even the Vice-President of the United States of America assuming supporting oppositional roles. Sometimes screenwriters are nervous of having a more ethereal antagonist and introduce secondary antagonists to embody the opposition for the audience. Thus in *Titanic*, whilst the iceberg was the antagonist, the makers felt the need to introduce a plotline that embodied opposition in the character of a jealous fiancé who then drove the actions of the principal characters up to the point of the ship sinking.

Catalyst – This character has a structure-centred role and is largely neutral in intention towards the protagonist. Their purpose is to present new situations that the protagonist has to respond to with action. It may be that they have little direct contact with the protagonist, and yet their actions impact directly.

In *Clear and Present Danger*, a secretary has an affair with an oppositional character. In a phone call to arrange an illicit liaison, she inadvertently reveals that her boss (a colleague of the protagonist) is on an unexpected trip to South America with the protagonist. Her revelation is the catalyst for an ambush and assassination that leads the protagonist to new and significant action, and clear character change and growth.

Perhaps more obliquely, in *Get Carter* (1971) it is Jack Carter's dead brother (a character the audience only meets in his coffin) who is the catalyst for the actions of both the protagonist (Carter) and the antagonist (Cyril Kinnear). Whilst having little direct contact, and certainly not undertaking direct action, he has considerable impact on Jack Carter's decisions, actions and reactions.

Supporting Characters – Whilst their primary function is to add levels of reality to the diegetic world, offering colour and detail, they are often more than just this. Some will be key in facilitating the direction of either protagonist or antagonist, while some will be structurally significant, acting as a bridge between scenes or signposting future events. In the television series *Cracker* (1993–5) DCI Charlie Wise was there to facilitate the direction of police psychologist Fitz and also to bridge scenes (particularly where Fitz was required to be off screen – either structurally or narratively).

Some supporting characters will be central to secondary (or sub) plots where they illustrate the themes and messages of the screenplay, and some will simply be functional – the characters you would expect to see in certain situations (a vicar at a wedding, a nurse in a hospital, a driver on a bus, etc.). Again in *Cracker*, DS Jane Penhaligon serves a key subplot which is an emerging love affair between her and Fitz, whilst DS Jimmy Beck is initially a functional character (hard bitten 'plod') who towards the end of the series evolves to be central to another subplot.

Voice of the Author Characters – Some characters are created to embody the themes and messages of the screenplay, and often their actions act as commentary on the actions of the other characters. They may even be given lines to illustrate the themes and messages (and the success of this depends on the skill of the screenwriter), and indeed, their sole function may be to deliver these lines. The successful US *Law and Order* franchise depends on such characters for each episode's ending, with the moral being spelled out for those who did not manage to get it from the action. Similarly in *CSI: Miami*, it is Lieutenant Horatio Caine who offers the writer's theme and moralistic comment in a final line at the end of an episode.

Minor Characters – Often non-speaking roles that are there to 'dress' locations and create a sense of *verisimilitude* (the sense of the 'real' – be that a 'real' saloon in Dodge City or a bar on a planet in a galaxy far, far away). A sense of verisimilitude is essential for the audience to be able to engage with the actions of the principal characters, and these characters facilitate the development of a scenic background against which story plays. *The West Wing* (1999-2006) is a great example of how this sense of verisimilitude is created through the placing of secretaries, secret service personnel, military figures, security guards, officials, clerks, cleaners, maintenance crew, tourists, etc. None of these are significant to the narrative, but without them colouring the background, the narrative effect would be lessened.

You should see that characterisation is significant in relation to the structuring of story and to the successful delivery of themes and messages. Like all activities involving the structuring of components there is an element of composition in which characters are placed in varying 'mixes' to achieve a pace and emotional depth to the screenplay. The placing of these various characters with their differing functions across the screenplay places emphasis on various elements at different times and changing the placing of one character can alter the 'feel' of the whole screenplay.

ACTIVITY

Fill in the Character Function chart (opposite). Think about what you are trying to achieve with the placing of characters and their functions. Try to avoid 'bunching' functions. Move the characters around to see what difference it makes.

CHARACTER FUNCTION CHART

Fill in the chart below with the details of who assumes what role in each scene. Remember, each scene may have its protagonist and antagonist – they may not necessarily be the main protagonist / antagonist.

Scene No	Location	Protagonist	Antagonist	Adjuster	Catalyst	Supporting Characters	Voice of Author	Minor Characters
44	Runway	Monica	'Tower' commander	Officer Rodriguez	Captain Kreig	Flight Controllers	Officer Rodriguez	Flight 303 Captain and First Officer

CHARACTER AND AUDIENCE

Characters, be they the Director of the CIA or the Slug Lord of Terramos 3, have to have the capability of connecting with an audience, which means that they need to be recognisable to that audience.

Identification is key to the way in which audiences use characters, looking for features in the characters, or character responses to situations, that remind them of the features or responses they are familiar with, either in people they know or (perhaps more importantly) in themselves. Seeing a similarity in character or response allows the individual spectator to connect to the character and identify with their plight and their solution to the plight.

When a character responds to events in ways that are familiar to an audience, there is opportunity for identification, even if the events are outside the spectator's experience. I know how I tend to deal with problems, be the problem the confusing choice of shampoos in a supermarket, or the way to destroy a Death Star; and so, if a character is responding in a way familiar to me, I may identify with them. Similarly, if a character faces problems that I am facing or have faced, I may identify with them.

When creating characters to populate a story, the screenwriter should have an idea of who the intended audience is. Cultural and even generational difference will influence the way that an audience responds to characters, and character actions and attitudes should be considered carefully to facilitate identification.

The primary focus of storytelling should not be structure, character, setting, dialogue or action, but instead should be audience. Without audience, the best story, the most skilfully created characters, the best drawn settings are nothing, since unless the audience accepts them, identifies with them and places them in relation to their own lives, then all of the screenwriter's skill is wasted.

[1] *Die Hard* official website - http://www.foxhome.com/diehard/trinity/dh1/

3. DIALOGUE

THE NEED TO SPEAK

You know, sometimes I think the Trappist Monks have it right. Their austere rule includes a vow of silence, and amidst the noisy chatter of modern life theirs seems the preferable route for the screenwriter. The need to speak is vastly overrated and for screenwriters the urge to 'tell' instead of show is a mortal sin that (like all sins) can be seen to be the solution to a problem (in this case, of structure), but is soon revealed to be a greater problem that in itself highlights a screenwriter's failings.

Contemporary screenwriters often justify dialogue as the only means of telling the story, but this argument neglects the history of the moving image. For the first 30 years or so of the moving image the screen was silent and story was expressed through *mise-en-scène* and through action (as the medium emerged intertitles were introduced to aid more complex storytelling). Audiences recognised and understood the actions of characters and were able to interpret the story from these. The argument that these stories were not complicated can be exploded by films such as *The Great Train Robbery* (1903), or even the frenetic *Keystone Kops* series where complex stories were played out with multiple characters – and not a word of dialogue heard.

The screenwriters then were confident of story and their stories worked – without words. They were confident in structure, confident in visual storytelling, confident in characterisation. They knew that their characters did not need to be heard in order to express what they needed to express – they had all the possibilities of a visual medium at their disposal and were in control of this medium. Many and often filmmakers have mourned the loss of this confidence with the introduction of sound and hence dialogue, and often dialogue becomes a constraint on the telling of story.

EXERCISE

Look at a favourite film or television show on your television. Turn the sound down and watch what is happening on screen.

Calculate the amount of time characters spend speaking, and the amount of time they spend in action.

Can you make sense of the story without the sound?

Now watch the next sequence with the sound back on. How much of the dialogue is pushing story forward, and how much is developing character?

How much story information is expressed through dialogue?

Dialogue has two roles in a screenplay:

Character function – Offering insight into character (background, thoughts, emotions, and behaviour).

Story function – Offering exposition (explanation or 'telling' of the story), commentary on off-screen events, and delivering backstory.

Bad writing usually forgoes character development in favour of excessive exposition; good writing is able to deliver both functions without one overly compromising the other; and great writing switches between the two seamlessly to the extent that it is almost impossible to identify which role is being serviced by a particular piece of dialogue (such screenplays include *Casablanca* (1942), *Witness* (1985) and *The Departed* (2006)).

Think about your favourite lines from a movie or a television show. From Humphrey Bogart's 'You played it for her, now play it for me', and Arnold Swarzenegger's 'I'll be back!', through to Homer Simpson's 'Doh!' and Matt LeBlanc's 'How you doin'?', all of these lines tell the audience about character, story or both. All of these lines have been carefully considered and constructed in order to serve a function in the screenplay, and as such have a significance way beyond the trivia of a pub quiz.

ACTIVITY

In groups, analyse a dialogue-driven scene from a screenplay for a film or a television programme of your choice. Consider the dialogue construction, the choice of phrasing, and the placing of the dialogue in the mouths of certain characters.

After discussing it line by line, take two highlighter pens and use one to identify all the lines for character, and another for all the lines for story.

Are there any lines that serve both?

Are there any lines that serve neither?

If so, what is their function?

Next, swap the dialogue between the characters. What difference does this make?

Lastly, as a group, rewrite the scene in language more familiar to your way of speech. What affect does this have on character or story?

In terms of character, the most essential task for the screenwriter is to find a character's 'voice' – the way they speak (phrasing), the language they use (vocabulary), any slang terms or jargon that categorises them (personalising), the pace and patterning of their speech (rhythm) and the reason for them opening their mouths (motivation). Initially, trying to write with these elements in mind can feel incredibly restrictive, but it does not take long before they become second nature to the screenwriter.

PHRASING

One of the funniest characters I have ever come across is the clothes shop sales assistant, Serge, in *Beverly Hills Cop* (1984). His affected manner, high pitched camp expression, bizarre accent and total informality creates a very strong secondary character. Yet if you swapped his character into the protagonist role, it would cease to be funny, as the way he speaks would quickly grate in a principal character.

Similarly, in *Friends*, making Joey a broad New Yorker lends a contrast to the middle class voices of the other characters. His accent and way of speaking help both to identify his character and to provide routes into potential storylines that would be blocked if he had another 'voice'.

VOCABULARY

A difficult challenge for screenwriters is that of putting words in other people's mouths. We all have our own sets of vocabulary that comes in part from our background, in part from our educational level and in part from the people we mix with both in employment and socially. A screenwriter has to go beyond their own way of speaking, in order to inhabit their characters and find the language they would use.

In the sitcom *Only Fools and Horses* (1981-2003), Del Boy over-extends his vocabulary in faux-French ('*mange tout*' to mean 'of course') and malapropism, and this is a primary indicator that his character is over-reaching and, to some extent, false. The dialogue here clearly stems from – and at the same time clearly reveals – his character.

The type of words characters use will often reveal their background. Just get a character to excuse themselves from a dinner in order to relieve themselves. What words do they use? Are they heading for the toilet, the bathroom, the loo, the lavvy or the john? Do they need to freshen up, hit the head, take a leak or have a pee? Each may not only say something about a character's background, but also about their relationship with others in the scene.

PERSONALISING

There is a real difference between someone who gives their address simply and someone who uses the International Radio Operator's Alphabet to spell sections of it out ('Postcode? Delta-Lima-three, five-Sierra-Oscar'). This use of jargon suggests a military or police background, and is likely to be reflected right though characterisation from haircut to type of clothing. Most occupations have forms of jargon that define them, and people tend to spill this jargon out from their working life unconsciously. Teachers will often refer to 'target setting', social workers to 'conditioning' and traffic wardens to 'penalties'. In *Prison Break* (2005-present) the characters' dialogue is liberally sprinkled with prison yard terminology (as would be expected) and this not only creates realism, but it lends a common bond between the characters.

Similarly with slang there are defining elements of language that place characters within certain sets or groups. A greeting that begins 'Alright, mate?' defines a character differently to one that begins 'Yo, bro!' or 'How do you do?'. Returning to *Sexy Beast*, the interplay between characters is made all the more 'real' by their use of slang and colloquialisms, the shared language not only of crime but of class. When discussing a 'job' with Gary, Don describes their common attitude towards crime:

DON

You're on two per cent, two and a half, maybe even three. Depends on the usual bumflufferies. It's not about the money with you and me is it, Gal? It's the charge, it's the bolt, it's the buzz, it's the sheer fuck off-ness of it all. Am I right?

The use of informality and restricted language 'the charge, it's the bolt, it's the buzz' defines the character speaking and the inter-relationship of characters.

It is worth mentioning here the significance of casual language – when US President George W Bush and British Prime Minister Tony Blair had a conversation, not realising a nearby microphone was live, it was not the detail of the conversation that was remembered but the relationship defining slang of Bush's greeting: 'Yo Blair!'.

This is where all of the lessons taught to us in English classes get overturned, as the screenwriter does not serve 'correct' language, but serves 'real' language. If screenwriters Louis Mellis and David Scinto were concerned with 'correct' language, then the above speech would probably have run something like:

DON

> Your share is two per cent, possibly two and a half, maybe even
> as high as three per cent. It all depends on the usual variables
> and imponderables. It's not about the money with you and me,
> though, is it, Gary? It's the thrill, it's the stimulation, it's the
> excitement, it's the sheer exhilaration of the criminal activity.
> Do you concur?

Not only is this a very different speech, but it makes Don a very different character, one whose actions we now might find more difficult to accept.

Language is personalised and revolves around groups (either occupational, social, class or regional) and in its personalising it defines the character. It is interesting to consider the way our language changes as our groupings change – often a core language set comes out when under stress, accents return, closed language returns and ways of speaking return.

RHYTHM

One of the keys to telling a good joke is the timing, the pacing and the delivery. This is the same with the dialogue in a screenplay. Consider the difference between the speech rhythms of the protagonists in *Forrest Gump* (1994) and *Jerry Maguire* (1996). One makes lethargy a virtue and the other maintains a high-octane delivery that requires stamina just to keep up. The rhythm of the language again reflects the characterisation and serves to confirm the view constructed by other character elements.

MOTIVATION

What makes you open your mouth to speak in any situation? A need to be heard, a need to show someone you have an opinion, a need to promote yourself, a need to impress, etc.? Whatever the reason, it can be reduced simply to motivation as the key.

Anything said by a character has to be motivated, either by their goal or by the situation. Motivated dialogue is crisp dialogue as it has a function and a focus. Unmotivated dialogue tends to be flabby and overlong since it has no *raison d'être* and no function to perform. Initially it is worth thinking about motivating a piece of dialogue or a speech, but as competence is developed this can be narrowed down to considering the motivation of single lines and even single words. If this seems extreme, think about your choice of language when you are annoyed – there is almost a hierarchy of offensive terms that are employed in relation to the situation and the recipient, a hierarchy that is motivated by context and audience. Thus, in *Aliens*, when the child Newt is threatened by the Alien Queen, Ripley says:

RIPLEY

Get away from her, you bitch!

Her expression is motivated not only by fear and anger, but by a protective, maternal instinct towards Newt. There is no need for her to say these particular words, but there is a need for her to speak, as she needs to attract the Alien Queen's attention away from Newt. The fact she speaks is motivated and the particular words are also motivated – this is well considered construction.

In terms of story, dialogue's primary aim should be to move the story forward, with a secondary aim of filling in backstory where necessary. It does this through revealing new information, creating conflict, revealing subtext and creating energy.

NEW INFORMATION

Every page of dialogue should present the reader with new information that moves the story forward. This could be character information ('I'm dying…') or it could be story information ('They're holed up in the forest, what's our next move?'), but either way it should not allow the story to remain static. If at the end of a page of dialogue the story has not moved forward, then that page of dialogue is not functioning as it should and is certainly not supporting the rest of the screenplay. Films and television programmes often sag at certain points and analysis can usually point to particular script pages where, however well written the dialogue is, new information is not presented and story is not being moved forward.

Three Days of the Condor (1975) is a movie about the survivor of the extermination of a CIA research office, and won the Edgar Allen Poe Award (given to movie and TV mystery writers) for the quality of its screenplay. Each and every page moves the story forward and reveals character, and the screenplay as a whole is a great example of writing. It is never static and never sags, presenting crisp dialogue that is constantly doing more than one thing, and is consistently working on several levels.

Below is a page from early in the draft screenplay that exemplifies the quality of the writing, the function of the dialogue and the detail of the structure:

INT. DOWNSTAIRS – RECEPTION AREA

The AAA-Arrow messenger is signing in for his pickup on Jennings' clipboard as TURNER comes up behind and gives him RAY'S envelope.

MESSENGER

Five pieces, right?

JENNINGS

Affirmative. Fiver.

The envelope goes into a dispatch bag. As TURNER starts towards the stairs, DR LAPPE comes out of his office carrying a sheet of paper.

DR LAPPE

Where is Mr Heidegger?

MRS RUSSELL

He called in sick, Dr Lappe.

JENNINGS

(mumbling)

Probably hangover again.

DR LAPPE

This is extraordinary. I was just checking the files and I found this carbon copy of an enquiry he sent to Persian Gulf Command.

Turner stops on the stairs.

TURNER

Oh ... he did that for me.

DR LAPPE

It never went through my office.

TURNER

Well ... I just asked him to do some research for me. I guess he thought it wasn't that important.

DR LAPPE

I wish you people would go though channels.

Suddenly TURNER's attention is caught by the TV monitor. He charges forward and out the doors.

Jennings is immediately revealed as having some form of military or government background though the language of his first speech – 'affirmative' is not a word that is commonly used by most people. His speech continues to reveal his character, especially when placed against the more formal and rigid speech of Dr Lappe. In terms of moving the story forward, both the carbon copy and Turner's inability to follow procedure has later significance. The dialogue on this page thus both reveals character and moves the story forward.

CONFLICT

If you listen to a conversation you will hear the parry and thrust of conflict, where subtle disagreements, long held grudges, simple differences of opinion and out and out enmity are played out. Two pensioners discussing their lunch can be a character assassination on a grand scale. Similarly, have a family get lost on a journey and see how quickly finding the right direction actually reveals the fault lines in their relationship. You should be able to detect conflict between Turner and Dr Lappe in the example above.

Conflict is story, and conflict-resolution is a motivator for moving story forward. Conflict in a scene will require future resolution that means additional scenes will be built on this one. Conflict expressed through dialogue places the conflict to the fore, and therefore provokes the need for resolution in the audience, moving the story forward.

Of course, conflict can be overly overt (through the use of bluntly focused 'on the nose' dialogue) and then has the potential to get bogged down in its own nature. Our own real world experience of conflict should tell us that it is quick to get into and slow to get out of. This is not possible in a screenplay where any scene that has run for three pages is heading towards an overly long scene (a page equals a minute), and where the conflict has to have a story or character role and so cannot afford to be self-serving. An example of conflict expressed both through dialogue and action comes in the police assault sequence in *Die Hard*, where not only the action demonstrates conflict, but the dialogue highlights four-way conflict between the terrorists, John McClane, Deputy Commissioner Robinson and Police Sgt Powell.

SUBTEXT

Our pensioners discussing lunch can be an exercise in presenting a subtext, where the dialogue presented is actually illustrative not only of the situation the characters are discussing but of situations from the backstory and also illustrative of character relationships (both past and future).

Get Carter features a now legendary telephone sex scene in which Carter (Michael Caine) sits in his landlady's living room talking on the phone to his lover (played by Brit Eckland) who is half naked and writhing on a bed. The dialogue is blunt and suggestive. However, it is the fact that the landlady is foregrounded, rocking back and forth in a rocking chair, which makes the scene as strong as it is in terms of delivering both story and character. Her blatant eavesdropping on the conversation and her suggestive action illustrates a subtext – the sexual tension that has been present between Carter and her since he arrived. The scene leads the audience to anticipate where their relationship will lead, and the screenwriter wastes little time in satisfying the audience's expectation.

ENERGY

Good dialogue is energised, but often there is a need to deliver expositional dialogue and this can deplete the energy. Returning to our pensioner's lunch critique, the obvious place for this dialogue is over the lunch table, but since the purpose of the dialogue is to reveal backstory and character, the lunch table may not be the only suitable venue for this. Let's transpose these characters to a railway terminus where they are running for a train, or a hospital where one is having an MRI scan, or even adjoining (and clearly competing) allotments. Suddenly what could be rather expository dialogue is energised and allows the subtext to rise through the scene.

In Episode 7 of *Band of Brothers* ('Breaking Point', 2001), two characters are in a foxhole discussing how their war has gone so far and where it looks like it is heading. Since the series is episodic and spans a lengthy period of time as the Allied invasion of Europe progresses across the continent, there was an expository need to locate the episode in its immediate time and place and to locate it contextually within a wider sense of the Second World War. These two characters in this particular scene are there to deliver the exposition. This could have been a fairly dull and static sequence, but the screenwriter opted to distance the audience from the characters part way through their discussion and place us in the position of an observer, with the inference that the observer is the enemy. They confirm this inference quickly by interrupting the discussion (once it has served its expository purpose) with a horrifically intense firefight, which moves the story forward and reinforces the characters' conversation through action.

EXERCISE

Note down (or, even better, record) 10-15 minutes worth of conversation. This real-world dialogue will be full of redundancy, as it does not have to meet the time limits of a screenplay.

Edit it down to no more than two pages of dialogue (this does not have to necessarily be delivered by characters modelled on the originators).

Energise this dialogue using a change of location.

How does the change of location inform character, story, and subtext?

How far removed from the original are your two pages of script?

PERCEPTION OF REALISM

Good dialogue writing gives the listener a sense of real world speech without actually including all the redundancies, stumbles and cut-offs that permeate everyday conversation. Just listen to a group of people talking, jostling for position, cutting in on each other, losing their thread and talking nonsense. Would any of that actually make a great screenplay?

Screenplay dialogue has a purpose with each line designed to push the plot forward and highlight characterisation. Simultaneously it needs to reflect (not replicate) the dialogue heard in our everyday lives, or the dialogue we would expect to hear in certain situations. It is this that helps create the perception of realism.

I have never been in the 'Situation Room' at the White House, on a Russian nuclear submarine nor in a space freighter heading back to earth after a mining expedition to our next nearest solar system. I've not been in them in reality, but in drama terms I have visited them hundreds of times through series like *The West Wing*, and films such as *The Hunt for Red October* and *Alien*. From work that has gone before, I have learned a perceived reality for such places and this allows me to shape my dialogue writing to this perception. Reality itself may be significantly different, of course, but the majority of the audience will not have been in any of these places either and so there is no need to become creatively stifled. A shared perception of reality is what is required to make good dialogue (and good screenwriting) work.

Some screenwriters turn this to their advantage. In Paul Attanasio's script for *The Sum of All Fears* (2002, an adaptation of the Tom Clancy novel) he has the President of the United States in the Situation Room with his advisors and general going through the protocols to launch a reactive nuclear strike. The dialogue is crisp and focused, as we have come to expect in the perceived reality of the Situation Room. Then, however, the President's phone rings and it is revealed that this is simply an exercise. Where it gets interesting, however, is in a later sequence after terrorists detonate a nuclear device and the President is facing a real nuclear strike launch. Here the President, and his advisors and generals, lose focus, worry about their actions, prevaricate and argue. The perceived reality is replaced by another perceived reality, but this one reflects the agony of decision making that we are all too familiar with (be it tensions at work or the arguments over a supermarket shopping trip). Suddenly we see the human side of those in office, those who are usually represented as being heroic and commanding; suddenly they are like us, facing uncertainty with the same fears.

ACTIVITY

Hand out scenes from screenplays that present a perceived reality that is likely to be outside the experience of those reading them (starships, vampire hunters, cavemen, sailors on a teaclipper, etc.).

In pairs discuss the perceived reality and explore how the dialogue is shaped to that reality. Note down the image it creates.

Individually rewrite the scene, changing only the dialogue, but presenting a different perceived reality through this.

Get writers to swap scripts and assess the new perceived reality. They should note down the image created by the new dialogue.

As a whole group discuss the way changing dialogue changes the perceived reality of the situation and how it can connect the perceived reality with particular audiences.

ACTIONS SPEAK LOUDER THAN WORDS

The key adage for screenwriting has to be 'don't tell, show' and this is probably truer now than in the early days of the visual media. As we spend most of our time talking to each other (on the phone, by text, by email and sometimes even in person) we have an over developed sense of description. Listen to people talking and you'll hear this in action. At the dinner table you are likely to hear 'Here's your dinner: chicken pie, mash, peas, and I've put some of that gravy on it that you like' as a plate of pie, mash, peas and gravy is put in front of you. At the petrol station when your car is the only one on the forecourt, you'll tell them which pump you used and will be asked in return 'Unleaded, 57 pounds and a penny?', only seconds after you've filled your car with 57 pounds and a penny's worth of unleaded petrol and they've watched you do it on their CCTV. When friends are round for a lazy day in the garden you'll walk out with a bottle of wine and enough glasses for everyone and announce 'Thought I'd open some wine, anyone joining me?' Outside the world of the screenplay we spend our time telling others what they can see we are doing.

The need to tell is ingrained in us and is a learned response to filling uncomfortable silences. It is one of the most difficult things for a screenwriter to unlearn. In screenwriting it has even acquired a special name – 'on-the-nose dialogue'.

On-the-Nose Dialogue is dialogue that is obvious, dialogue that telegraphs the action:

> Franco lies dead on the floor, his body riddled with bullets, a knife sticking out of his heart, an empty bottle of poison beside him, and a thirty-eight ton truck's wheels parked across his head. Louie walks over to the body and looks it up and down slowly.

LOUIE

> Looks like he's dead.

* *

> Mary angrily reaches across to the drinks cabinet and pulls out a bottle of gin and a glass.

MARY

> I'm so angry! I need a drink!

* *

Corporal Marceaux marches his troop of Foreign
Legionnaires across the sun bleached, barren desert. He
pauses and removes his hat wiping the dripping sweat of his
burning face.

CORPORAL MARCEAUX

(sighs heavily)

Phew, it's hot!

The novice screenwriter (and to a lesser extent the experienced screenwriter) usually includes much on-the-nose dialogue in a first draft of a screenplay. The skill here is to recognise it as such and take action to rewrite the dialogue (or even better, just let the action speak to the audience and excise the dialogue altogether). As a rule of thumb, if dialogue is merely repeating what has been shown, or is stating what is being shown then silence is definitely preferable.

Look at the sequence below from the film *Syriana* (2005). The screenwriter Stephen Gaghan presents an action sequence that could easily involve a great deal of declamatory dialogue, but instead is stripped down and what dialogue there is, is either cut off or is counterpoint to the action. The sequence continues with Mr Janus entering into a lengthy congratulatory speech that serves to highlight the ruthless and vicious military execution.

195. INT. BRYAN'S VEHICLE. DAY   195

Bryan stares ahead. His POV up the length of the convoy. The
HUM of the highway. He turns and sees, out of the window, the
Mitsubishi SUV cutting towards them.

                                        CUT TO:

196. INT. CIA TASK FORCE BUNKER. NIGHT   196

ANGLE – MONITOR

The toy-like convoy snakes across the desert. Another car
enters the frame, angling towards the convoy.

FRANK (O.S)

What's that other car?

                                        CUT TO:

197. INT. PRINCE NASIR'S HUMMER. DAY   197

The SCREAMING baby takes the bottle and quiets. Prince Nasir makes eye contact with his wife and smiles.

A bodyguard in the front hears something over the radio and points out to the desert –

Nasir turns and looks at Bob's car fast approaching –

                                                    CUT TO:

198. INT. MITSUBISHI SUV. DAY   198

Bob angles the car in tighter, waving the white flag.

Nasir's bodyguards point their weapons.

                                                    CUT TO:

199. INT. PRINCE NASIR'S HUMMER. DAY   199

Prince Nasir sees him. They make eye contact –

A bodyguard begins shouting into a walkie-talkie. Other vehicles race forward and surround Bob's car, forcing it to stop.

200. EXT. DESERT HIGHWAY. DAY.   200

Soldiers with their weapons on Bob. He steps from his car holding the white shirt in front of him

(CONTINUED)

200. CONTINUED: 200

                        BOB

        It's okay. It's okay.

Bob slowly approaches Prince Nasir's vehicle. They stare at one another. Nasir lowers his window.

                    PRINCE NASIR

        I remember you. You're the Canadian.

Tight on Bob. He starts to speak –

A WHITE FLASH

                                            MATCH CUT TO:

201. CIA TASK FORCE BUNKER. NIGHT   201

ANGLE – MONITOR

A TINY POOF of white smoke. And vehicles scatter in crazy

Syriana

directions. Then a rush of black smoke.

ANGLE – THE ROOM

The crowd of Chiefs and Technicians erupts into celebration, handshakes, and high fives.

ANGLE – MONITOR

The tendril of black smoke is spreading into a black cloud. The vehicles are stopped.

CUT TO:

202. INT. BANQUET HALL – OIL MAN OF THE YEAR. NIGHT
202

The room is silent. Mr. Janus stares into the crowd.

> **MR JANUS**
>
> I accept this award on behalf of the employees of Connex-Killeen, our people, the finest in the world ...
>
> *(moved)*
>
> Guys, could I get you to stand up for a moment?

At the CONNEX table, Tommy and Jimmy and the others get to their feet. The crowd APPLAUDS. Bennett applauds Jimmy who sees him clapping and applauds him right back –

EXERCISE

Take the pages of script you wrote for the last exercise (based on recorded conversation) and see if you can strip most of it away by replacing it with action.

What have you lost by cutting the dialogue? What have you gained?

REFLECTIONS OF CHARACTER

Dialogue has another key function that is vital to get right. Dialogue is a method of delineating character, not only through what is said, but by the *way* it is said and the language employed to say it. Think about the sequence in *Four Weddings and a Funeral* (1994), where Charles (Hugh Grant) chases Carrie (Andie MacDowell) along London's South Bank in order to declare his love. There are countless ways for him to do this, but writer Richard Curtis takes the opportunity to further reinforce his characterisation by having him stutter and hesitate:

CHARLES

(hesitant)

Ehm, look. Sorry, sorry. I just, ehm, well, this is a very stupid question and... , particularly in view of our recent shopping excursion, but I just wondered, by any chance, ehm, eh, I mean obviously not because I guess I've only slept with 9 people, but-but I-I just wondered... ehh. I really feel, ehh, in short, to recap it slightly in a clearer version, eh, the words of David Cassidy in fact, eh, while he was still with the Partridge family, eh, "I think I love you," and eh, I-I just wondered by any chance you wouldn't like to... Eh... Eh... No, no, no of course not... I'm an idiot, he's not... Excellent, excellent, fantastic, eh, I was gonna say lovely to see you, sorry to disturb... Better get on...

CARRIE

That was very romantic.

CHARLES

Well, I thought it over a lot, you know, I wanted to get
it just right.

Similarly in an exchange of dialogue there is the opportunity not only to clarify individual characterisation, but also the relationship between characters, as in David Lynch's *Blue Velvet* (1986), where Jeffrey meets Frank for the first time:

FRANK BOOTH

Hey you wanna go for a ride?

JEFFREY BEAUMONT

No thanks.

FRANK BOOTH

No thanks? What does that mean?

JEFFREY BEAUMONT

I don't wanna go.

FRANK BOOTH

Go where?

JEFFREY BEAUMONT

For a ride.

FRANK BOOTH

A ride! Now that's a good idea!

Here can be seen a building block of the characterisation of relationship, which is where dialogue can take the screenplay to a new level. We see the rise of one character over another and the sense of a new question developing: where will Frank take Jeffrey, and what will become of him? The way that Frank manipulates the situation by twisting round Jeffrey's dialogue gives a clue to the deviousness and lurking menace that becomes all too apparent later in the screenplay. The way that Jeffrey is subdued and easily manipulated confirms much of what has been learned about him so far.

EXERCISE

Review the openings of some of your favourite films. Note down the first lines of dialogue that the protagonist delivers. Does it have special significance?

Using a character sheet, write the opening lines your character says in your screenplay. These are the first words that your audience will hear your character say, and should give them a sense of who the character is.

MAKING DIALOGUE WORK

Writing dialogue is usually the last stage in the process of writing a screenplay before the rewriting process begins, and is often the most difficult activity for a screenwriter. Indeed, in the industrialised writing processes of Hollywood, it is not uncommon for one writer to construct the screenplay up to the point of dialogue and then for another to take over specifically to write the dialogue. Some screenwriters even make a living just writing dialogue.

Dialogue functions in three ways. Firstly, it articulates characterisation and as such is significant in allowing an audience to identify with characters. Secondly, it articulates story through the discussion of what is happening in or around the scene. Thirdly, it articulates theme, often through snippets of moralising dialogue. In Callie Khouri's *Thelma and Louise* (1991), Louise finds Thelma in the car park of a bar struggling with a would-be rapist and pulls a gun on Harlan, the attacker:

LOUISE

Get off her or I'm gonna splatter your brains all over this nice car.

HARLAN

[Getting off of Thelma]

Easy, we're just having a little fun.

LOUISE

Sounds like you got a real fucked up idea of fun. Turn around. In the future, when a woman's crying like that, she isn't having any fun!

Louise's last line here articulates precisely the theme of the film – how men mistreat women through ignorance or contempt. But here the moralising is concealed by the fact that the scene is driven by conflict and is dominated by action. What could have been clumsy dialogue that announces an obvious moral issue becomes instead the believable, natural-sounding lines that an angry and frightened woman may well come out with in such a situation.

Here are ten tips to making dialogue work:

1. Keep it short and keep it simple. Better to have short staccato exchanges of dialogue rather than Shakespearean monologues. Similarly, if you are writing a biopic about Albert Einstein the language used must be understandable to the average audience member (of an average audience, not one of Nobel prize-winning physicists).

2. No lengthy speeches. Whilst established screenwriters can pretty much do what they want, when you are starting out lengthy speeches will be seen as the mark of the amateur. The logic behind this, however, is that long speeches generally slow down action and therefore slow down the pace of the screenplay. A lengthy speech can be hidden, however, under action, under a change of place or a change of time (in both of the latter cases the speech links a montage of images).

3. Attach expositional, character or moral dialogue to action in order for it to seem less 'visible', less obvious.

4. Individualise speech. Each character should speak with a distinctive 'voice' and should have a distinctive vocabulary to match.

5. Avoid writing in colourful dialect – directors and actors will be able to add and adapt any linguistic variety the screenplay demands. If you have a Scottish character then tell the reader that they are Scottish and then leave them to read your crisp non-dialect inflected dialogue. They'll read it with an accent, and anything else will be determined by dialogue coaches when it comes to production.

6. Avoid on-the-nose dialogue (see above).

7. Consider the rhythm of speech. Speeding up, slowing down, pausing, etc. are all ways of regulating dialogue and are ways of making dialogue less flat. Careful punctuation will allow actors to express these rhythms appropriately.

8. Allow reaction and thinking time. When a character delivers an important piece of information other characters will react, but the initial reaction should not offer a fully formed response or plan, as these both require some time to consider. Better to break the scene on the revelation and then come back to the response in another scene.

9. Use reaction shots instead of dialogue. Getting characters to nod, look shocked or even wet themselves in terror is usually preferable to dialogue responses to a situation.

10. For every line of dialogue consider whether there is a better way of saying it, a later point in the speech to start, an earlier point in the speech to end, and where in the scene the individual lines should come.

ACTIVITY

Get each group member to bring in a few of their longer dialogue scenes. Hand these out to the group members so that nobody gets their own work.

Using the dialogue tips above, each group member should write an analysis of the scenes they have in front of them, noting recommendations for changes and suggestions for improvement.

Allow time at the end of the session for each group member to feed back to the screenwriter whose work they analysed. If possible, attempt to collect together common dialogue problems, and discuss as a group how these can be avoided or rectified.

4. STRUCTURE — FROM IDEA TO FORMAT

In Chapter 4 you will be introduced to the following:

- Story versus plot.

- The three-act structure.

- Alternate structuring.

- Generating ideas and concepts.

- Synopses and treatments.

- The extended step-outline.

- The master scene script.

- Openings and endings.

STORY VERSUS PLOT

Central to structuring any story for the screen is the idea of plotting. Plotting is the ordering of those elements of story that have been narrativised (remember, narrative is those parts of the story selected to be included or told).

Story is the tale to be told, whilst plot is the way of telling, and like all good recipes, it is the way the ingredients are assembled that can make the difference between success and failure. Let's remind ourselves of our earlier definition of plotting:

Plot is the ordering or positioning of the elements (or narrative), the mixing up in order to create dramatic tension, to promote a viewpoint or to show authorial ingenuity. Plot is the way the story is told from opening to ending, and through all the many choices in between.

The selection of material is often difficult and it is usually useful to have an idea of how you intend to assemble the material as you make the selection. However, it is similarly useful to have a little more material than you will need to construct the screenplay in order to allow you to edit down (this is considerably easier than adding at a later date).

The easiest way of understanding plotting is that all stories are structured with a beginning, middle and an end. Aristotle identified this thousands of years ago when he wrote *Poetics*[1] to advise writers how they might structure (or plot) their stories. Central to his theory were two plot phases, those of complication and of resolution.

Complication is the placing of obstacles in the way of the protagonist's goal. A character should be set in conflict with another character, with themselves or with a situation, and this conflict should be developed through a series of complications.

Resolution recognises the need for the obstacles in the way of the protagonist to be overcome so that they can progress towards their goal. In order to satisfy audience expectation most screenwriters set out to resolve conflicts at the end of the screenplay.

It is only natural for conflict to intensify, as more and more obstacles are negotiated and more and more complications arise until the conflict reaches a crisis. Think about how playground arguments progress, how family rows escalate (especially on long car journeys) and how wars start. Characters (just like the people around us and ourselves) have ambitions, desires, emotions and egos, and as soon as you place them in situations of conflict, these human attributes cause them to react, and to continue reacting up to and through the point that the conflict reaches a climax.

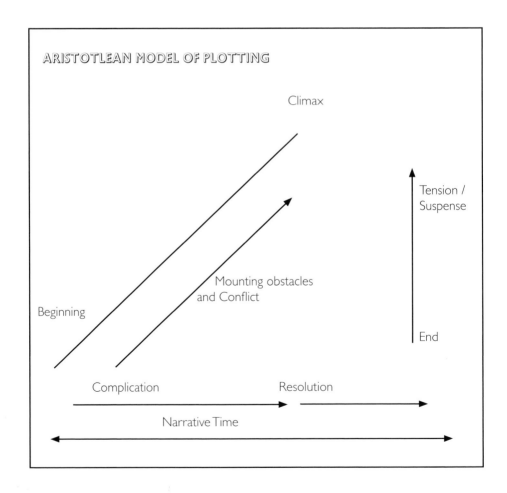

ARISTOTLEAN MODEL OF PLOTTING

Climax

Tension / Suspense

Mounting obstacles and Conflict

Beginning

End

Complication

Resolution

Narrative Time

You should be able to see from the above model that the level of tension and suspense rises towards the climax and then falls off sharply as the conflict is resolved. This could also be modeled as increasing audience involvement with the narrative and with the characters, rewarded with a sharp emotional release. This is sometimes termed a cathartic moment – the point where the identification and involvement provokes emotion and release that spills over into real life, provoking a similar emotional release. The emotional release produced from the fictional world connects with 'real world' emotional needs of the spectator and may provoke a corresponding 'real world' emotional release. I cry for the turmoil in George Bailey's life in *It's a Wonderful Life* (1946), but at the same time I am also crying at the recognition of the turmoil in my own life – a cathartic moment caused by identification and involvement.

In *Syriana* the audience is led to identify with Bob, Bryan and Prince Nasir, and the suspense is ratcheted up with each scene until Prince Nasir's convoy is hit by a CIA airstrike just as Bob is about to warn him and tell him of the circumstances he has found himself in. The shock of the success of the airstrike is a cathartic moment, provoking strong reaction in the audience. From this point (pages 123–5 of the 129 page screenplay) the suspense falls off sharply as the script enters its final phase of resolution.

EXERCISE

Look at the model opposite. Take a screenplay you are familiar with (preferably one that has been produced) and map the model to it. Note down what page the climax occurs.

Now take a second and third screenplay and map the model onto them. Again note where the climax comes.

Is there a pattern forming? If so, why do you think it is?

Do you feel that this model is sufficient for a contemporary screenplay? If not, what else should go on the model?

If you have suggestions, redraw the model.

You may have thought that the upward line of conflict and obstacles is a little too smooth and one-directional. If an obstacle is placed in the way of a character do they simply continue on their path and 'roll over' the obstacle, or does it cause the character a setback? A setback may provoke a backwards movement, or a stall in momentum, which, whilst overcome, means the one-directional movement is interrupted.

Similarly, you may have noticed from your exploration of the screenplays that conflict does not immediately happen at the start of the narrative, but happens once the audience has been given time to become familiar with the characters and their situations.

With this in mind, the model might be modified as follows:

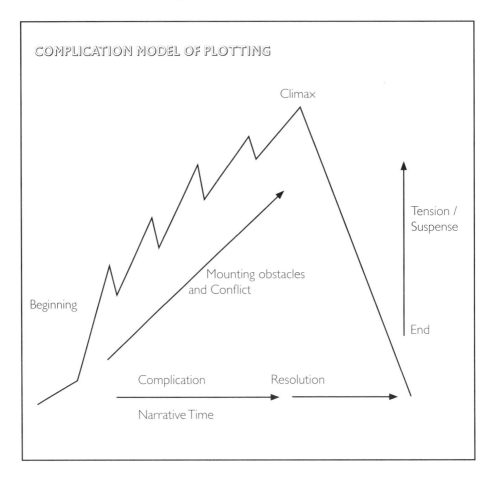

COMPLICATION MODEL OF PLOTTING

Climax

Tension / Suspense

Mounting obstacles and Conflict

Beginning

End

Complication   Resolution

Narrative Time

If you look at the resolution phase of the plot, as the screenplay moves to its conclusion, you may notice that the original model is again not quite sufficient for the modern screenplay. As resolution begins there is often a final resurgence of the antagonist who will place one last obstacle or reversal in the way of the protagonist. This one will test the protagonist, but will be overcome quickly (even though it may be challenging). In the final moments of *Die Hard* the terrorist Karl rises up from the ruined remains of the Nakatomi Plaza and points his gun at the unarmed John McClane and his wife Holly Genero. The audience tension immediately rises only to have this tension instantly dissipated by Sargeant Al Powell bringing him down with a single shot.

This delivers a three phase model of plotting: a **set-up phase** that sets the scene and gives the audience a familiarity with the characters and the situation; a **development phase** in which the protagonist and antagonist struggle as the protagonist is faced with decisions, obstacles and self-doubt; and a **conclusion phase** where all of the plot lines are resolved (unless a sequel is planned) and where the goal of the protagonist is achieved (largely). But this is in reality just a refinement of what Aristotle originally proposed:

Beginning – the set-up: What is the protagonist's goal and what do they have to do to achieve it?

Middle – the development: Conflict ensues, and the protagonist acts and reacts to the obstacles placed in their way. Their journey to get what they want happens across this phase and the focus of this is struggle. It is in this phase that the character will face a **mid-point crisis**, where they will learn something about themselves after obstacles and failure, and this will enable their renewed struggle towards the climax.

End – the conclusion: a final push towards resolution and the fallout from the conflict. This is where the character realises their goal (this may actually be different from what the character thought they wanted).

David Griffith looks at plotting from a very industry-focused, practical approach in his *A Crash Course in Screenwriting*[2] when he writes:

Screen stories are all about questions and answers. At the story level you must ask:

• What is my story really about?

• What do I want to say?

• What is the story's big hook?

• What makes it cinematic (or televisual)?

• Why is it way better than anything else I've seen?

• Would I pay to see it?

At the character level you must ask:

• Complication (*his term for the development phase*)

• Setup

• Who is my lead character?

• What do they want?

• How can I show what they want?

• What do they need to learn about the world or themselves in order to get what they want?

• How can I demonstrate visually what they need?

Increasing Conflict

• Who opposes them?

• How do they attack the lead character and expose their weaknesses?

• Why is the lead character resistant to change, reluctant to confront their weakness?

• How does the level of conflict increase?

• What makes the conflict personal?

• Does the conflict become obsessive and force even friends to start deserting the lead character? (if not it should!)

• How is the lead character finally forced to confront their weakness and contemplate internal change?

Unraveling (*his term for the conclusion phase of plotting*):

Resolution

• Why does the lead character come back for one last attempt to defeat their opponent?

• Do they still want what they did at the beginning, or are they beginning to understand that they will never win unless they change their goal or their attitude to life?

• What moral choices that they have to make in the final struggle will finally externalise their inner struggle between what they want and what they need?

• How does the lead character close the divide between what they want and what they need in the climax and resolution of the movie?

Returning to the screenplay, assuming the screenplay is a two-hour feature film, the set-up equates to around the first 30 pages (a page of screenplay is calculated at approximately one minute), with the central character and their goal established within the first 10 pages. The development phase will cover approximately 60 pages, and the last 30 pages cover the resolution phase. In Hollywood, script reader reports are often divided into these section breaks, and the page formula for plotting is seen as a mark of professionalism. The most important thing is that there is a beginning, middle and an end, and that there is not an overweighting of the set-up or resolution in relation to the development phase (as this will mean that action is lost).

Thus, for the 112 page script of *Casino Royale* (2006), the character and goal are established by page 12, the set-up concludes on page 27, and the resolution phase begins when James Bond is wheeled into hospital on page 90. This approximates the above model, and allows the writer to see that working to a model need not be restrictive, as it is clearly not an exact science.

For television the structure is different as most programmes are significantly shorter than two hours and in the majority of television the need for advertising revenue (and hence ad breaks) drives the structure. Largely (in drama, though this carries across to other televisual forms) a screenplay will be divided up into a number of acts (often four to six depending on the number of anticipated ad-breaks), with each act ending in a crisis, an obstacle for the protagonist to overcome in order to ensure the audience returns after the break. The return sees the obstacle overcome, or a new direction taken to solve the crisis, coupled with a forward momentum towards the final act, the resolution. Take a look at any popular television show such as *The Bill*, and you'll see how page accurate this model is – the demands of a television schedule mean that there is less structural freedom than in film.

ACTIVITY

Split a group into small discussion groups.

Take Dave Griffiths' questions and have the group members question each other about their screenplays / ideas.

Take the opportunity of revising the narrative, the plot, and the characters, then rotate the members of the groups to new groups so the new ideas and new directions can be interrogated.

Screenwriters should identify the journey of the screenplay across the two sessions of questioning, and should be able to restructure their work in the light of comments.

THE THREE-ACT STRUCTURE

The three-act structure is an established form in mainstream screenwriting, and it is essential that you are aware of how it works and why it works (even if you don't want to be restricted by its constraints). Some screenwriters feel restricted by such structuring of what they see as a purely creative activity, but alternatively it could be seen as a liberating force, taking the structural burden away and leaving the screenwriter free to deal with the creative interpretation of story.

The three-act structure is a model that has evolved out of successful screenwriting. It offers a formula that is carefully focused on moving the narrative forward within a mainstream industrialised format, with specific events or incidents required to happen on specific pages. It is punctuated by backstory, inciting incidents, plot points, setbacks, and actions and reactions.

> **Backstory** – This sets the scene and lends 'reality' to a diegetic world, and may offer the historical context of events, of a situation, of a time, of a place or of a character. Good screenwriting presents some of the backstory at the start of the screenplay (in the first act – enough to allow the audience into the diegetic world), and then sprinkles it across the screenplay through the action, the *mise-en-scene*, the dialogue and the characterisation. Poor screenwriting offers backstory in expository, signalled 'chunks', usually through dialogue. Possibly the best example of the delivery of backstory comes in *Sunset Boulevard* (1950) which begins with the narrator dead in a pool, presenting his backstory, that leads up to the main storyline, that in turn leads to his death in the pool.

Sunset Boulevard

> **Inciting incident** – This is an action, event or piece of dialogue that provokes change in the protagonist's circumstances, and sets them on a journey to resolve the ensuing conflict. This can sometimes seem innocuous, and it is only on reflection that it can be

seen as being at the root of the narrative journey (the cracking ice shelf at the start of *The Day After Tomorrow* could be lost under the dramatic special effects that dominate the plot, and yet this clearly signals the change that provokes the characters' actions throughout the rest of the film).

Plot points – These are the moments that turn the narrative in a different direction and may be the result of specific actions, of dialogue or of a change in the situation. In *Deep Impact* (1998), the first plot point is the discovery of the comet heading for Earth – this springs the narrative to life, and characters to action. Another, later, is the revelation that most people will be abandoned to their fate, changing the behaviour and attitudes of characters. The plot point that comes just prior to the crisis point is the impact of the comet. Plot points are the springboard for change in a screenplay.

Setbacks – If a character's momentum towards resolution were straightforward, there would be little interest in their journey. A character's momentum must be interrupted by setbacks, short-lived reversals that force them to re-evaluate their planned course of action. Again, in *Deep Impact*, the government takes action to destroy the comet, but their action fails and they have to face the enormity of the consequences of this reversal.

Actions and reactions – Plot points are designed to provoke actions to address the change of direction in the narrative. Characters are stirred into courses of action that they would not have necessarily pursued had something not changed the direction of the narrative. With their course of action set, they then face setbacks that in turn provoke reactions in which they discover things about themselves, and adjust their chosen course of action to allow for the change of circumstance forced on them by the setback.

These are placed within three sections that correspond to the plot phases identified above.

Act One: Exposition (a set-up and a complication)

This section introduces the characters and locates them within their 'normal' world. This world could be that of a detective in a dystopian future (*Blade Runner*), or of a mix-up at the Ministry of Education leading to a girls' school being forced to board at a boys' school (*The Happiest Days of Your Life* (1950) – the origin of the St Trinian's movies). It establishes the characters' 'normal' abilities in their 'normal' situation.

In this act there is an inciting incident that provokes or initiates a change in the protagonist's situation, marking the beginning of the narrative journey. A plot point near the end of this act is the springboard into act two, and signals the point of no return for the protagonist.

Act Two: Development (obstacles, setbacks, and a crisis)

In this act the protagonist goes on a journey that is beset with obstacles and setbacks, as they attempt to resolve their conflict and achieve their goal. At the start of act two the antagonist's intentions are revealed and the two parallel storylines are propelled towards an inevitable confrontation and crisis. Needless to say the protagonist's goal and the antagonist's intentions are diametrically opposed, in order to create further conflict and opposition (if they were not, there would be little in the way of conflict since both could achieve what they want without impeding the other – not much drama in that!).

The protagonist will face a mid-point crisis of self-revelation where the course of action to resolve the complication and conflict becomes clear, and they make a decision that will influence the rest of the narrative. In modern Hollywood films this has taken on a focus on the emotional or psychological that points more to a contemporary cultural obsession than any significant structural rationale. Thus in *American Gangster* (2007) drugs dealer Frank Lucas burns the fur coat he was persuaded to wear by his wife, as he realises this has placed him on the drugs squad radar (with the potential to lead to his demise) and more importantly realises that he has broken his own rules.

The act ends with a confrontation with the antagonist that leaves the protagonist in a crisis (this could be an external crisis – such as hanging off the side of a building – or could be an internal one – such as the belief that there is no way to resolve the conflict and defeat the antagonist). This is usually the plot point that springs the narrative into the third act. Leaving act two, the protagonist has usually hit rock bottom, with their situation significantly worsened, and probably as bad as it could get.

Act Three: Solution (a final confrontation and then, resolution)

This act restarts the protagonist's journey towards resolution and has near its beginning a further confrontation with the antagonist, which results in victory for the protagonist. The rest of act three is all about resolving the storylines that have been introduced earlier and producing closure in order to leave no question unanswered. The protagonist's situation is resolved and they achieve their goal (even if it is not the one they thought they were heading for).

Some films use the final moments of act three to set up a sequel, and this is usually achieved by leaving a storyline unresolved. Poor scriptwriting may set up the sequel by introducing a new storyline at this point, just to introduce the elements that will form the basis of the subsequent screenplay.

EXERCISE

Structure Analysis – this is a method of assessing whether each of your three acts is doing what they are supposed to do.

Act One: Does this act set up the central characters and their situation? Does it establish conflict, by setting out the protagonist's goal and introducing the oppositional force?

Act Two: Does the second act produce increasing complications that build cumulatively towards the crisis at the end of the act? Does suspense / tension increase measurably across this act? Is the protagonist presented with increased jeopardy, and do they respond with heightened urgency? Is there a clear climax at the end of the act where the protagonist meets the antagonist in confrontation?

Act Three: Is the central conflict resolved by the end of this act? Are there any storylines / questions left unresolved / unanswered? Has the protagonist achieve their goal? Has the antagonist been beaten? Is the ending satisfying, or is it tired and expected?

Lastly, look at how you have moved from act to act, the transitions. Are they seamless and story-centred, or do they reveal the structural intentions? Is cause and effect evident, logically bridging the acts, or do the transitions reveal screenwriter convenience?

ALTERNATE STRUCTURING

There are countless alternatives to the three-act structure, put forward by theorists and screenwriters (some having successfully written screenplays and worked in the industry, and others with a book to sell). Dancyger suggests a character-focused structure in *Alternative Screenwriting: Writing Beyond the Rules* (1991), and Phil Parker similarly focuses on character development as a means of structuring story in *The Art and Science of Screenwriting* (1998).

However, a model that I have found particularly interesting and useful in the practice of screenwriting is Michael Hague's Six Stage Structure[3], which identifies six stages dividing up a screenplay, structured by five key plot points. Instead of being preoccupied with the details of time and quantity of pages for each section, he talks in terms of the percentage of a plot, which allows this to be scaled for any form, from the short to the feature.

Stage 1 – The Set-up

This follows the same rationale as the set-up in the three-act structure but only represents 10% of the screenplay. At the 10% mark, the protagonist is presented with an opportunity (Plot Point 1) that initiates a desire in the protagonist. This is not the introduction of the protagonist's goal, but probably equates to the inciting incident.

In Joshua Marston's *Maria Full of Grace* (2004), just before the 10% mark Maria quits her job and at the 10% mark she is made aware of her poverty and need for money. It is this that drives the rest of the film.

Stage 2 – The New Situation

Taking the opportunity places the protagonist in a new situation. This may well be a change of physical location – the start of a journey – or it may be a change *within* a physical location (such as a house getting bulldozed) and the next 15% of the screenplay deals with the protagonist coming to terms with the new situation and planning how they are going to achieve their goal. At the 25% mark, the protagonist is faced with a dilemma that provokes a change of plans (Plot Point 2). This change of plans clarifies their goal and what they have to do to achieve it.

In *Maria Full of Grace* over the next 15% Maria begins her search for ways of making money, and these lead at the 25% mark to her being introduced to Javier who runs drug mules. She is faced with a dilemma and her decision changes both her direction and that of the film.

Maria Full of Grace

Stage 3 – Progress

Moving the plot through to the halfway mark, the model sees the protagonist succeeding in the path they have chosen, and progressing with their plan to achieve their goal. The obstacles the protagonist faces do not greatly hinder and are either quickly overcome, avoided or their consequences postponed. This section concludes at the 50% mark with a point of no return (Plot Point 3), where the protagonist makes a decision that prevents them going back and leaves them with only one option – moving determinedly forward towards their goal.

At the 50% mark Maria has stepped off a plane and into a US airport, where she waits to go through customs. She follows the set of lies she has been given, as she has no option at this point but to move forward with the plan.

Stage 4 – Complications and Higher Stakes

The next quarter of the screenplay is where it gets tangibly more difficult for the protagonist to achieve their goal. Conflict multiplies and complications become more challenging to overcome. It is in this section that the concept of jeopardy is introduced and what the protagonist risks is made clear. At the end of this section (exactly 75% through the screenplay) the protagonist will face a major setback (Plot Point 4) where it seems that they have been defeated. It is at this point that the antagonist has taken centre stage and is at their strongest. The protagonist is left with no other choice but to make a final bid – win or lose – to achieve their goal.

In *Maria Full of Grace*, this section begins with Maria being detained by Customs just at the point she thought she was free. Her fellow mule is x-rayed and arrested, but Maria is released as she is pregnant and cannot be x-rayed. Escaping the US end of the smuggling ring (after they kill another of the mules in order to get the drugs out) without her payment, she goes to stay with the dead mule's sister, lying to her in order to be taken in. At this point, Maria has taken a path and seems defeated.

Stage 5 – The Final Push

This section moves the plot through the final 15–24%. The protagonist has to risk all to win all, and the conflict is at its greatest. The odds are stacked against the protagonist and every turn is met with new complications and new obstacles. These reach their height with a climax (Plot Point 5) that comes around the 90–99% point in the screenplay. This is where the protagonist faces their biggest obstacle and confronts the antagonist. In this model the placing of the climax is determined by how much time is needed for the final section of the plot.

The discovery of the dead mule's body results in Maria's involvement being revealed to the sister she is staying with, and she is evicted. Forced onto the streets she has no money and no choice but to take the drug 'pellets' back to the smuggling ring to see if she can get her money. Facing them down, she gets her money, but it is a clear choice between this and being killed.

Stage 6 – The Aftermath

Interestingly, this section (that can come anywhere from 90 to 99% of the way through the screenplay) begins with the victory of the protagonist, the point where they achieve their goal. The rest of this section deals with establishing their new life, their new situation and their new state of mind.

Maria uses some of the money to pay for the dead mule's body to be returned to Columbia. She then resolves to return home and pick up life as a mother.

ACTIVITY

Form pairs and issue each pair with a screenplay from a major feature film.

Using Michael Hague's model get each pair to work their way through the scripts finding the pages the plot points fall on.

Do the pairs produce similar results? What can be learned from this?

Get each pair to produce a plot point grid, listing what is happening in the screenplay at the points the five plot points are reached.

GENERATING IDEAS AND CONCEPTS

It is likely that the first screenplay you write is one that is based on something that has inspired you and that you have become passionate about, be it issues around the Iraq war, issues around social security 'scroungers' or issues around growing old. Passion will drive the story development, and passion will aid the structuring of the plot.

However, not all scripts start with inspiration and passion, and as screenwriting becomes a career rather than something done in your spare time, there will be a need to generate ideas and concepts for screenplays, as regularly and effectively as electricity is generated. For some people ideas flow naturally and they can deliver them as if on a conveyer belt. For others the process can be painful and stifling.

There are two places I go when I need to kickstart creativity and generate story ideas and concepts: firstly, proverbs (common popular sayings) and, secondly, to the work of Georges Polti.

PROVERBS

The list below is by no means exhaustive, and there are hundreds of other common wise sayings (some of which have biblical origins in the Book of Proverbs) and thousands world wide from diverse cultures (again many of them based in religious mythology). But this is a list that I have used to stimulate my imagination and to provide a context for a story to grow, or a plot to emerge:

1. A bad penny always turns up.

2. A bad workman always blames his tools.

3. A beggar can never be bankrupt.

4. A bow long bent grows weak.

5. A bully is always a coward.

6. A drowning man will clutch at a straw.

7. A fair exchange is no robbery.

8. A fool and his money are soon parted.

9. A friend in need is a friend indeed.

10. A great fortune is great slavery.

11. A guilty conscience needs no accuser.

12. A lie begets a lie.

13. A lion's skin is never cheap.

14. A new broom sweeps clean.

15. A pennyweight of love is worth a pound of law.

16. A small leak will sink a great ship.

17. A stick is quickly found to beat a dog.

18. A word spoken is past recalling.

19. A wise man changes his mind, a fool never will.

20. A thief knows a thief as a wolf knows a wolf.

Of course, having these may not stimulate *you* – but a simple online search will reveal many, many more lists. Some, such as Number 17, seem rather obscure, but if considered then not only their meaning is revealed, but the practical truth of them stirs stories – with this one I am already thinking about witch-hunts, victimisation and the hysterical rule of the mob; thoughts that can lead me from the French Revolution, through Salem and Rwanda, to present day Iraq.

You can see how this works with traditional proverbs, but here are some contemporary spins on proverbs that reflect our modern world. Try some of these out for size:

1. Those who live by the sword get shot by those who don't.

2. The things that come to those who wait are usually the things left by those who got there first.

3. Everyone has a photographic memory. Some just don't have film.

4. The 50-50-90 rule: Anytime you have a 50-50 chance of getting something right, there's a 90% probability you'll get it wrong.

5. He who laughs last, thinks slowest.

6. I just got lost in thought. It was unfamiliar territory.

7. Nothing is foolproof to a sufficiently talented fool.

8. Seen it all, done it all, can't remember most of it.

9. I started out with nothing, and I still have most of it.

10. Everybody lies, but it doesn't matter since nobody listens.

GEORGE POLTI'S THIRTY-SIX DRAMATIC SITUATIONS

George Polti (a nineteenth century French theatre critic) analysed hundreds of plays and novels spanning the preceding centuries in order to demonstrate that there are only 36 situations for use in constructing a drama. His book *Thirty Six Dramatic Situations* appeared in English in 1920, and he subsequently published *The Art of Inventing Characters* in which he identified 36 character types for use in drama.

All situations in any story or drama are supposed to fall into one of his 'dramatic situations', and 'situations' can be applied in multiples to help create and structure a work. I've used these often to stir my imagination, and I have also experimented with combinations to stimulate a more dynamic structuring of the resulting story.

There is no particular order to them, other than the way Polti wrote them down. Number 1 is no better that Number 36. All suggest the situation from which a story can develop, and many have an inherent plot inferred from them. The key to their use is to not take them too literally, and not to get too caught up in fulfilling the specific, identified roles in them.

1. **Supplication**
   Elements: a Persecutor; a Supplicant; and a Power (authority figure), whose decision is questionable.

2. **Deliverance**
   Elements: an Unfortunate, a Threatener, a Rescuer

3. **Crime Pursued by Vengeance**
   Elements: an Avenger and a Criminal

4. **Vengeance Taken for Kindred Upon Kindred**
   Elements: Avenging Kinsman; Guilty Kinsman; Remembrance of the Victim, a Relative of Both

5. Pursuit

Elements: Punishment and Fugitive

6. Disaster

Elements: a Vanquished Power; a Victorious Enemy, or a Messenger

7. Falling Prey to Cruelty or Misfortune

Elements: an Unfortunate; a Master or a Misfortune

8. Revolt

Elements: Tyrant and Conspirator

9. Daring Enterprise

Elements: a Bold Leader; an Object; an Adversary

10. Abduction

Elements: the Abductor; the Abducted; the Guardian

11. The Enigma

Elements: Interrogator, Seeker and Problem

12. Obtaining

Elements: a Solicitor and an Adversary who is refusing, or an Arbitrator and Opposing Parties

13. Enmity of Kinsmen

Elements: a Malevolent Kinsman; a Hatred or reciprocally Hating Kinsman

14. Rivalry of Kinsmen

Elements: the Preferred Kinsman; the Rejected Kinsman; the Object

15. Murderous Adultery

Elements: Two Adulterers; a Betrayed Husband or Wife

16. Madness

Elements: Madman and Victim

17. Fatal Imprudence

Elements: The Imprudent; the Victim or the Object Lost

18. Involuntary Crimes of Love

Elements: the Lover, the Beloved; the Revealer

19. Slaying of a Kinsman Unrecognised

Elements: the Slayer, the Unrecognised Victim

20. Self-Sacrifice for an Ideal

Elements: the Hero; the Ideal; the 'Creditor' or the Person or Thing Sacrificed

21. Self-Sacrifice for Kindred

Elements: the Hero; the Kinsman; the 'Creditor' or the Person or Thing Sacrificed

22. All Sacrificed for Passion

Elements: the Lover; the Object of the Fatal Passion; the Person or Thing Sacrificed

23. Necessity of Sacrificing Loved Ones

Elements: the Hero; the Beloved Victim; the Necessity for the Sacrifice

24. Rivalry of Superior and Inferior

Elements: the Superior Rival; the Inferior Rival; the Object

25. Adultery

Elements: a Deceived Husband or Wife; two Adulterers

26. Crimes of Love

Elements: The Lover; the Beloved

27. Discovery of the Dishonour of a Loved One

Elements: the Discoverer; the Guilty One

28. Obstacles to Love

Elements: Two Lovers, an Obstacle

29. An Enemy Loved

Elements: The Beloved Enemy; the Lover; the Hater

30. Ambition

Elements: an Ambitious Person; a Thing Coveted; an Adversary

31. Conflict With a God

Elements: a Mortal, an Immortal

32. Mistaken Jealousy

Elements: the Jealous One; the Object of whose possession he is jealous; the Supposed Accomplice; the Cause or the Author of the Mistake

33. Erroneous Judgement

Elements: The Mistaken One; the Victim of the Mistake; the Cause or Author of the Mistake; the Guilty Person

34. Remorse

Elements: the Culprit; the Victim or the Sin; the Interrogator

35. Recovery of a Lost One

The Seeker; the One Found

36. Loss of Loved Ones

A Kinsman Slain; a Kinsman Spectator; an Executioner

It doesn't take an enormous leap to see how some of them apply to existing screenplays (No. 35 – *The Searchers* (1956); No. 33 – *The Hand that Rocks the Cradle* (1992); No. 9 – *Kellys Heroes* (1970); No. 2 – *28 Weeks Later* (2007), etc.), but some of them take a little more effort than others, and a technique that may be useful is to 'translate them', thus No. 13 ('Enmity of Kinsmen') becomes:

Hostility in a family

Elements: an evil minded family member; a cause of ill will, or two family members that hate each other.

This could certainly be the basis for many a screenplay for nightly soap operas.

ACTIVITY

1. Make a list of proverbs and cut them into individual 'proverb strips'. Get group members to select one and in no more than five minutes come up with as many screenplay ideas as possible.

Get them to repeat the exercise with another 'proverb strip', and then have them share their screenplay ideas.

Discuss how 'visually dramatic' these ideas are. Explore ways of visualising them.

2. Give one of Polti's 'Dramatic Situations' to each person in the group and have them spend no more than three minutes sketching out an initial idea around it.

Next, share the ideas and see if any have the potential for combining, discussing their similarities and underlying dramatic potential.

Form small discussion groups around ideas that have similarities, and allow up to ten minutes to develop the ideas into a synopsis for a screenplay. Share the ideas and then vote for the one with most potential – with group members having to justify their vote.

There is a clear similarity between Polti's inspirational one-line 'dramatic situations' and the contemporary practice of producing 'loglines'. A logline is a two-sentence description of the story behind the screenplay, and is designed to be a 'selling' tool; therefore, it needs to engage and entice the reader or listener, and should make them want to read the synopsis, the treatment and hopefully the whole screenplay.

A logline delivers a view of the story, often from the point of view of the protagonist, and is focused on offering a succinct summary of their perception of events. Thus, the logline for *The Terminator* (1984) may read:

Sarah Connor faces execution at the hands of an indestructible cyborg sent back in time, because she will be the mother of the man who (in the future) will save humankind from destruction when the robots rise.

It can be inspirational to take loglines for existing screenplays and re-write them from another point of view. The logline for *The Terminator* when expressed from the Terminator's point of view could be the starting point for a whole new film:

> A cyborg is sent back in time to kill the woman responsible for a (future) threat to order and stability on Earth.

The logline is effectively the premise, on which the synopsis is built, from which a treatment grows and eventually a screenplay is born, so it is worth considering and phrasing these carefully.

SYNOPSES AND TREATMENTS

The construction of a screenplay should always follow a process of moving from the general towards the particular, and so it begins with a premise (or logline) that is expanded upon in the synopsis. The synopsis is a succinct summary of the screenplay plot and is usually between 200 and 600 words, depending on the length of the proposed screenplay and the complexity of the plot (where the plot is particularly complex it may be best to offer a simplified version in the synopsis).

The synopsis is a 'selling' tool that is designed to stimulate enough interest for the reader to want to read (or, better, commission) the treatment. It is sometimes used as a calling card in the hope that it will result either in a sale of a speculative screenplay, or in the commission of a specific piece based on the talent shown in constructing a synopsis. It should be noted that a good synopsis takes as much crafting as a screenplay.

The synopsis you will create for the constructional purpose of producing a screenplay will not be the same one that is presented to a potential buyer / commissioner. For our immediate purposes I am talking about a synopsis whose sole purpose is to crystalise the essence of the proposed screenplay, to distill its unique flavour and to organise your thoughts on a page. As the story moves through the other steps towards the conclusion of the process, elements will be refined and changed, so the synopsis will need to be rewritten before it is used as a sales tool.

Sample Synopsis – *Pirates of the Caribbean: At Worlds End* (2007)

It is a dark time as the Age of Piracy nears to a close. Lord Cutler Beckett of the East India Company has gained control of the terrifying ghost ship, the Flying Dutchman, and its malevolent, vengeful captain, Davy Jones. The Dutchman now roams the seven seas, unstoppable, destroying pirate ships without mercy, under the command of Admiral Norrington.

Will Turner, Elizabeth Swann and Captain Barbossa embark on a desperate quest to gather the Nine Lords of the Brethren Court, their only hope to defeat Beckett, the Flying Dutchman, and his Armada.

But one of the Lords is missing—Captain Jack Sparrow, either the best or worst pirate ever, and now trapped in Davy Jones' Locker, thanks to his encounter with the monstrous Kraken.

In an increasingly shaky alliance, our heroes, including Tia Dalma, Pintel, and Ragetti, must first travel to dangerous, exotic Singapore and confront Chinese pirate Captain Sao Feng to gain charts, and a ship, that will take them off to world's end, to rescue Jack. But even if Captain Jack is successfully rescued, the gathering of the legendary Brethren Court may not be enough to hold back the fearsome tide of Beckett, Davy Jones and their powerful Armada... unless the capricious sea goddess Calypso, imprisoned in human form, can be freed and convinced to come to their aid.

As betrayal piles upon betrayal, it becomes clear that Jack, Will, Elizabeth, Sao Feng, and Barbossa each have their own agenda, and no one can be trusted. Yet each must choose a side, and make their final alliances for one last battle, in a titanic showdown that could eliminate the freedom-loving pirates from the seven seas – forever.

The synopsis leads to a further expansion into a treatment. The treatment is a step-by-step walk through the narrative and is both a plotting tool and a 'selling' tool. This is a much less hard and fast document that can range from two or three pages to 90 pages, and can be in a prose style or in a sectionalised form.

A currently popular form is to use headings covering **concept**, **characterisation**, **theme**, **tone** and **story**. It is interesting that this is an industry-driven format that places story last and concept first (the concept is, of course, what an audience is first exposed to in marketing material, so there is some industrial logic to this).

Examples of treatments can be found across the Internet, and the three following treatments are representative of the range available:

Mr & Mrs Smith Treatment

This treatment runs to 1800 words, covering six pages, and uses the contemporary style mentioned above.

http://www.creativescreenwriting.com/csdaily/SmithsTreatment.html

Batman Year One Treatment

This Wachowski brothers' treatment for a proposed feature runs to 1200 words covering 4 pages. It uses a succinct prose style and is a good prose model for a straightforward plot.

http://leonscripts.users5.50megs.com/scripts/BATMANYEARONEproposal.htm

The Terminator **Treatment**

James Cameron's epic treatment runs to 17,000 words over 55 pages in a very detailed prose style. Cameron can get away with this style of treatment because of his status as a Hollywood director – you will not be able to. If you are writing a treatment of this length, you are misdirecting your energies and should concentrate on the screenplay instead.

http://www.scifiscripts.com/scripts/Terminator_Treatment.txt

THE EXTENDED STEP-OUTLINE

The step-outline is a scene-by-scene walk through of your script idea where you can get a sense of who is on screen for what amount of time, how scenes work next to each other, whether a scene is the right length or not and where the balance of action sits. It is an incredibly useful tool in terms of getting the structure of the story right before you waste too much time writing scenes you will eventually have to discard or rewrite.

I used to use 4"x 6" cards and pin them up onto a board so that I could physically see the structure of the story, but there was often not enough information on them so they then began to be accompanied by post-it notes and scraps of paper. With this in mind I started using an extended step-outline sheet (see page 109) that can include significantly more detail beyond just a description of the scene. Some of it is simply obvious information such as scene number and endpoint of last scene, but other parts will need a little explanation if you are to use them to the full:

Point of Scene: I cannot stress enough how important this piece of information is, since if you are unable to come up with an answer to this then you have your answer – there is no point and it should be deleted. The point of a scene may be character based (to allow the audience to learn something about a character or to see an action that informs them what kind of character this is), or it may be story based and largely expository (there to deliver a piece of dialogue or action that reveals story aspects). It can be there solely to draw out an emotional context, or to provoke an emotion in the audience (think 'the little girl in the red dress' element of *Schindler's List*). It can, however, also be legitimately structural, fulfilling the need to bring two characters together, or to place an obstacle in the way of a character.

It is important to write it down, so you can see the balance between types of scene. Too many structural scenes and the audience will not engage with character. Too many character based scenes and the audience will not engage with the story.

Character goal: What is the principal character in the scene trying to achieve? Is it something physical, emotional, intellectual? Is it part of an overall goal or is it something more immediate? If it is part of the overall goal, how will that be shown on screen without it weighing too heavily on the scene? If it is something more immediate, will it be resolved by the end of the scene (this is important to consider, as otherwise you will need to check through subsequent scenes to ensure that at some point this goal is either achieved or abandoned, otherwise the audience will have a doubt nagging at them that will disturb their engagement with the material).

Conflict: All scenes should have conflict whether it is the epic struggle between man and god, or the lesser struggle of trying to get the lid off a jam pot. Conflict is the essence of story and should therefore be the essence of a scene. If a scene lacks conflict then it lacks dramatic tension, and if it has no dramatic tension then it will need either deletion or a re-write. It is often simple to resolve in largely expository scenes by having the characters involved in an activity that lends action to the 'telling' (an old man telling his grandson how he single-handedly won the war could be relatively flat until you have him simultaneously struggle to take the lid off a jam pot – suddenly there is conflict that produces characterisation and pathos).

Twist: Is there a twist to the scene? A twist is usually something unexpected or outside of what is anticipated and can come through action, dialogue or *mise-en-scène*. It is useful to consider this, as a twist is often what generates energy in a scene, and so becomes a driving force for drama.

This may be a twist in character, where a character either voluntarily does something out of character (thereby revealing their true character – possibly against audience expectation, as in *Terminator II: Judgement Day* (1991), when the Schwarzenegger Terminator is revealed as being a 'good' cyborg instead of the 'bad' cyborg expected from watching the previous film), or where they are forced to do something out of character (see *Sophie's Choice*, where a mother is forced to choose between which one of her children will be killed by Nazis).

Ending: How a scene ends is probably more important than how it begins, as the end of a scene is where its real strength lies. Scenes all too often go on too long and peter out instead of ending at a key moment – a dialogue revelation, an emotional reaction, a story progression, an action that reveals characterisation or a prop plant (where we are shown a prop that will become relevant later).

A scene usually answers a question set in a previous scene, with characters in the new scene trying to resolve the question set in the previous scene(s). The principal characters in the scene struggle to resolve the question and in the process set a new one. The new scene will usually end when one of the principal characters in the scene sets this new question, a question that requires a change in location or in time to provide the answer. This question drives the story forward into the next scene where the audience expect the question to be answered.

Scenes build into sequences, sequences build into acts and acts build into the total screenplay. Each unit has its own question attached to it. A scene has a question that leads to the next question and the next scene. The scenes build to a sequence that has its own driving question that is answered by the next sequence as they build towards an act. The act is driven by a question that is answered in the next act through to the end when the resolution answers the final question (franchise screenplays use the resolution either to leave a question partially unanswered or to raise a new question that will be answered by the sequel).

ACTIVITY

Show the group several sequences from a film or television programme that should be reasonably familiar to them (show enough sequences so each sub-group can look at one).

Break the group into sub-groups and give them one of the sequences to use for an analysis / discussion. Firstly get each group to try to find what is the key question that their sequence is asking, the key question that drives the sequence.

Once this is done, they should break the sequence down into scenes and discuss how each scene sets up a question and what ways these questions are answered in successive scenes. What ends the sequence and how does it lay the ground for the next sequence?

Looking at the step-outline sheet (opposite) you will see that half the page is given over for a scene description and it stresses 'without dialogue'. The reason for this is to give you space to describe the setting and what is going on without worrying about what is said or how it is delivered. This allows you to visualise the setting and the action without reliance on dialogue carrying the scene (something that happens all too often), and means you will be focused on *mise-en-scène*, on sound, and on how it might be shot (although this is not directly your concern, it should be on your mind and if it is then you can write a scene to suggest the way it should be shot).

A typical step-outline sheet may run like this:

Slugline:	*Ext: Riga Camp. Day*
Endpoint of Last Scene:	*Lina and Rosa crawl under the barrack hut*
Characters in Scene:	*Roschmann, Abrevenko, Schröder*
Point of Scene:	*To show Roschmann's realisation that he has lost control*
Character goal:	*To prove he is still in command*
Conflict:	*Roschmann's desire to flee set against his need to lead*
Twist:	*The death of Abrevenko at Schröder's hands*
Ending / central question:	*Roschmann forced to flee with Schröder / What will become of Roschmann?*

Scene No		Page No		
Slugline				
Endpoint of last scene				
Characters in scene				
Point of scene				
Character goal				
Conflict				
Twist				
Ending / central question				

Scene description (without dialogue)

Scene Description (without dialogue): *Shells are now landing inside the camp and the prisoners are running desperately from the barracks, and opportunistically jumping from the trucks. A guard opens up with a machine gun and a group of prisoners are caught in the gunfire. They dance like marionettes. As Roschmann's open-topped staff car pulls into the camp yard in a cloud of dust, one of the barrack huts takes a direct hit and explodes into splinters of wood. Roschmann's car skids to a halt. Roschmann stands and begins barking orders, waiving his pistol in the air. Schröder climbs slowly from the car, head bleeding from shrapnel as Abrevenko runs over to report that the guards are beginning to break ranks and flee. Abrevenko is rabid and encourages Roschmann to show his command. Roschmann leaps from the car and grabs hold of a retreating guard, slapping him and forcing him back in the direction he came. As Roschmann moves into the rear of the scene, towards the trucks and the huts, Abrevenko throws himself on a retreating Kappo, placing his pistol to the frightened man's mouth. A shot rings out and Abrevenko is thrown sideways. Schröder has shot him. An explosion rips through a truck in the rearground and Roschmann is caught in the blast. He stands unsteadily, defeated. Schröder runs to him and helps him to his feet where he dazedly looks around the chaos of the camp. Schröder pulls Roschmann away and they join the exodus*

EXERCISE

Take a film or television programme that you like and watch a sequence of between five and ten scenes. You should choose an opening sequence, an end sequence, or a key sequence where the story is moving forward dramatically.

Using the step outline sheets break the sequence into scenes and fill out the template for each scene. Concentrate on defining what the central question for each scene is and how that is answered in subsequent scenes.

Do you notice that the scenes work without dialogue? Dialogue should amplify what is already in the scene, and the scene should be just as strong without it.

From this example, not only do I know what kind of scene it is and what kind of characterisation I need to write in, but I am also already beginning to think about the dialogue I may employ. Since I am starting from a position of scene description rather than screenplay, the dialogue should now be more sparse and tighter than if I wrote it alongside the description.

Writing an extended step-outline means that you are thinking visually and, therefore, are likely to be less reliant on dialogue when you come to write the screenplay. Any script editor will tell you that the biggest part of their job is removing unnecessary dialogue, and this process will make you very popular with script editors.

THE MASTER SCENE SCRIPT

The Master Scene Script is a layout that is recognised as professional across the industry. Both film and television layouts are exemplified below, but the common thing with both is the absence of camera direction.

Camera direction (framing terms – CU, MS, LS, etc. – camera movement – CRAB, TRACK, CRANE, etc. – and in-shot changes – ZOOM, PULL FOCUS, CANTED ANGLE, etc.) is strictly the province of the director and cinematographer, and so should be avoided. It is easy enough to infer a shot and, if it is absolutely necessary there is nothing to stop a screenwriter suggesting a particular shot to create a particular effect, as long as this is very infrequent. Similarly with editing instructions: there is little point in ending each scene with CUT TO, as that is the screenwriting equivalent of telling someone to breathe. Occasionally there may be the necessity to offer a particular instruction such as a DISSOLVE or a FADE OUT for dramatic or constructional reasons, but these should be placed in the knowledge that a director or editor may well decide to remove them. One such instruction that is seen as valid for a screenwriter is MONTAGE in order to connect a range of disparate shots together (particularly when compressing time).

The purpose of the Master Scene Script is to give a clear 'feel' for the diegetic world and for the story. It should provide a clear and detailed description of each scene, clear identification of the characters, and their speech and intonation at particular points. It is a document that when read should 'play' in the mind. When I read a good screenplay, the movie runs in my head; locations become so real I feel like I'm there and characters become lifelike and human. The movie that plays is, of course, my own *envisioning* of the screenplay and not that of the screenwriter, although based on the screenwriter's. This is because the Master Scene Script is a plan, a blueprint of how the story should appear on the screen.

Using the right layout may seem ridiculous to the novice screenwriter at first, and an inconvenience. However, it is essential that the format is adopted from the moment you commence your screenplay, as this will, firstly, save you time at a later point (there is nothing worse than having to re-format a screenplay), and, most importantly, will make the right impression on agents, producers, directors and production companies. If you demonstrate an understanding of industry formatting, it suggests you may also have an understanding of industry styles and conventions, and therefore your screenplay is probably worth looking at. No matter how good the content, a screenplay that is in a significantly different format is unlikely even to get into the pile to be read (most Hollywood studios receive over 200 screenplays a week, and the BBC drama department receives over 60 television plays a week). That's not to say that the brilliant screenplay in an unusual format will not be recognised as wonderful once it is read, but unless it is read that brilliance will never reach the screen. The most useful visual clue to professionalism is writing the screenplay using Courier 12 font, as this allows the length of the screenplay to be measured, allowing for approximately one page of manuscript to equal one minute of screentime.

SCREENPLAY FORMATTING

Covers, front pages and bindings: Screenplays are usually presented with a buff, beige or white front cover (and matching rear cover) that either has a title window cut into it or a title label stuck to it. The whole package is hole-punched and secured with brass fasteners. No one will be concerned with fixing you to these exact details, but a screenplay should be presented largely in this form as it shows an awareness of industry norms. Glossy, brightly coloured, attention seeking covers and / or bindings are to be avoided at all costs.

The front page should be relatively minimalist offering at the top left a description of what the package contains – Feature Film Screenplay / Documentary / Television Sitcom, etc. – in order for a reader to immediately see on arrival whether it fits their current requirements. You need to make things easy for readers to accept your screenplay, as they are the first of a series of gatekeepers that sit between you and your success. Centred vertically and above the centre line horizontally should come the title and the author name. There is no need to add anything else here (readers have little concern over who you are, just what you have written). In the bottom right hand corner comes the author's name, address, contact telephone numbers and e-mail address. These details are duplicated on the final page of the screenplay (the reasoning here is that it is possible a front or rear cover may go missing, but unlikely that both will). In the bottom left should come the date of submission – month and year only.

Front Cover Layout

Type of screenplay

(Feature Film / Sitcom etc.)

The Rip Off

By

(your name)

Your Name

Your House No & Street

Your Town

Your Country

Your Postcode

(your country if needed)

Your Telephone Numbers

Date: September 2007   Your e-mail address

The Screenplay page

The film Master Scene Script uses a single column format with wide margins. Pages should be numbered consecutively in the top right of the Header, and in the bottom right of the Footer the letters 'mf' should appear to indicate that 'more follows'. On the final page of script the Footer should have the word 'Ends' centred. Screenplays should always be single sided.

The first page of script will have the title of the screenplay centred and in capitals at the top of the page. Below this on the left of the page in capitals should be the words FADE IN: – all film screenplays start in this way as a long-standing convention (even if a fade in is not the way it is intended to start).

From this point onwards, all pages of script will use identical formatting.

Each scene begins with a heading called a Slugline. This Slugline provides vital information for the technicians who will create the scenes.

SCENE NUMBER: Scenes are numbered consecutively in UK / European master scene scripts, but when submitting to the American market the scene numbering should be removed. The Scene Number appears at the start of the Slugline and is replicated on the same line on the far right of the page – this is to allow ease of finding scenes when using a bound screenplay.

INT: Interior settings tend to be those that would need artificial lighting – this could be in a room, in a car, in a cave or even in the stomach of a whale.

EXT: Exterior settings tend to be those that would have natural lighting or re-creation of natural light – this could be a street scene, on the deck of an ocean liner or in deep space.

INT/EXT: This is used to describe a location that is either between interior or exterior (such as a doorway), or when the scene contains both (such as a setting where two characters are conversing at a car window, with one inside the car and one outside).

LOCATION DESCRIPTOR: This should be simple, descriptive, succinct and, most importantly, constant – if you call the same setting a 'lounge' in Scene 1, a 'parlour' in Scene 10 and a 'front room' in Scene 23, you will undoubtedly cause confusion.

DAY/NIGHT: This is a descriptor for scheduling purposes that allows the production manager to work out what lighting crew are required and what a day's schedule might look like. There is no need to offer alternatives such as DAWN or DUSK unless it is significant to the scene (in the vampire film *Near Dark* (1987) the descriptors SUNSET and SUNRISE had particular significance to the action of the scene). Occasionally this can be followed by a time descriptor (such as a date – 3 SEPTEMBER 1939, or 09.30h), but this is again only needed where it offers particular significance to the scene.

If a scene continues over a page, then in the bottom right of the page the word 'continues' should be abbreviated as (CONT:). At the top left of the next page the abbreviation CONT. should appear without parenthesis and without the colon.

Below the Slugline comes the Scene/Action Descriptor. This is where you describe what is happening in the location described in the Slugline, using the present tense. When you first use a location (or if it has significantly changed since you used it last) you should offer some *mise-en-scène* description to set the scene. This should be kept relatively short and should only include anything relevant – if you are describing a suburban street, this term is probably enough to conjure up an image and should only have added detail (burnt out car in the middle of the road, one of the houses painted bright pink, etc.) where it is significant to the scene. After this has been suggested once, it need not be mentioned again unless it changes.

Similarly, when a character is first introduced they should have a succinct description to aid the rest of the characterisation. This should ideally be no more than a couple of lines and, of course, should only cover physical description (only describe what can be shown on screen). The first time a character appears in a screenplay their name is capitalised, but after that it remains in lower case. Generally it is best to use the name that the characters themselves will use – this could be a full name, a surname, a first name or a nickname, but whichever it is it must remain constant throughout the screenplay. Even minor characters should be defined with a name if only to differentiate them, and lend a degree of characterisation: there is a world of difference between character names POLICEMAN 1 and GRUFF POLICEMAN.

The Scene Descriptor should identify the key action of the scene, and will reappear between pieces of dialogue (and may appear between lines of dialogue if an action is happening as someone speaks – in this case the dialogue is broken, the description is inserted on a separate line, and then the dialogue begins again under the character's name with '(cont.)' after it).

Any essential camera instruction should appear in the scene descriptor in capitals (e.g. TRACK IN), and any essential edit instruction should appear on the right of the page in capitals, followed by a colon (e.g. DISSOLVE TO:).

Dialogue should always appear under the name of the speaker and this should be centred and in capitals. The dialogue itself should be indented consistently (one centimeter at each end is sufficient), and any instruction as to how a line is delivered should appear in italics and parentheses under the character name. If a character directs their speech towards another character mid-speech then this should be indicated in italics and parentheses within the body of the dialogue.

FILM SCRIPT LAYOUT

12. EXT. OUTSIDE THE AIRLOCK. DAY.   12.

BRYCE staggers towards The Pallentine, barely able to see
its flashing airlock lights through the wind whipped
sandstorm. He lopes forward pulling a makeshift stretcher
carrying the lifeless bodies of HANCOCK and SYED.

13. INT. BRIDGE OF THE PALLENTINE. DAY.   13.

HATCHER slumps in the Captain's chair, as the console in
front of her flickers with lights. Staring down at a
screen mounted on her armrest, her finger reaches out to a
joystick and toggles the menus: Oxygen Levels, Fuel Cell
Levels, Hull Status. At Lander Escape Window a clock reads:
00:00:10:12. She watches it count down.

From under the flight control desk emerges FOURIER,
springing to his feet and rapidly moving his hands across
the desk, flicking switches and watching the darkened
flight screens surge into life. A smile spreads across his
face. It quickly disappears when a monitor flicks on and
he spots Bryce outside. He reaches out to turn it off.

                                              DISSOLVE TO:

14. EXT. OUTSIDE THE AIRLOCK. DAY.   14.

Bryce reaches the airlock, rests the stretcher, pauses for
a beat, before raising his arm and, pressing a button on
his control panel. Looking up at the unresponsive door he
presses it again with increasing anxiety.

15. INT. BRIDGE OF THE PALLENTINE. DAY.   15.

A red light flashes across Hatcher's face as the screen
displays "Start Launch Sequence Immediately"

                         HATCHER
                       (anxiously)
          Damn it, Bryce! (to Fourier) Go for launch.
                                              (CONT:)
                                                  mf

THE TELEVISION SCREENPLAY

The television screenplay uses a double column format that has the script written on the right hand half of the page, leaving the left hand half for director, talent and crew to make the notes relevant to themselves to aid with the visualisation of it.

The binding and front / rear page of the screenplay is identical to the film Master Scene Script format, and it again has the same Header and Footer information. It is titled in the same way, but thereafter the form begins to differ.

Television screenplays are divided into Acts and these acts are identified on the page, with an underlined heading in upper and lower case (e.g. Act One). The following Sluglines are in lower case and are underlined, though they follow the same format as the film Master Scene Script Slugline (with the exception that the Scene number is not repeated on the right of the page).

The Scene Descriptor follows the same format as the film Master Scene Script format, with the exception that the character names remain capitalised throughout.

Dialogue is fronted by the character name capitalised and left aligned in line with the Slugline and Scene Descriptor, and intonation is expressed in parentheses behind the name. Word emphasis is expressed by underlining in the dialogue.

EXERCISE

Using the information above and the templates for both film and television screenplays, write the first five pages of your screenplay.

Once finished, go back through what you have written and trim out any unnecessary words and phrases. Be particularly harsh with dialogue, cutting any 'on the nose' dialogue and any overtly expository dialogue.

Look at this edited screenplay (you may have excised between a third and a half of what you originally wrote). Is it still understandable? Does it still manage to convey the story? Is it better or worse than the original?

TELEVISION TWO COLUMN SCRIPT LAYOUT

4. Int. Bar. Evening.

LANCE and GREG burst through the door laughing and stumble down the four steps into the bar area.

GREG (shouts): 'Ave it!

LANCE (laughs): Large!

The move to the bar and Lance bangs the flat of his hand down.

LANCE: Tequilas: <u>six</u> of them!

5. Ext. Street. Evening.

A low black sedan sweeps round a corner and slows on the wet street, growling towards the bar.

6a. Int. Bar. Evening.

LANCE and GREG slam their tequilas down on the bar and then drink them back.

6b. Int. Bar toilets. Evening.

LANCE falls through the door and barges into BUSINESSMAN at urinal.

6c. Int. Bar. Evening.

LANCE and GREG slump at a table. GREG rises unsteadily and then is violently sick down himself.

mf

OPENINGS AND ENDINGS

The opening of a screenplay is a key point of decision for a reader that you have managed to persuade to open the front cover, and so should be one of the areas worth most attention from the screenwriter. An opening should immediately set the tone and grab the reader, whilst introducing the situation and the central characters. Openings are notoriously difficult to get right, and are often (along with endings) the section of the screenplay that receives the most re-drafting. If a reader has not 'got' your screenplay within the first ten pages, then it is unlikely that they will continue to read on.

There are three things that should be achieved in an opening:

Introducing the protagonist – Where the reader can get a picture of who the central character is, what their situation is and what kind of responses they are capable of. The protagonist is usually introduced in one of two ways; either in the middle of an action (as in *Stake Out* (1987), where the central characters enter the story as cops chasing a villain) that reveals their context and their dominant attitude, or as part of a community that they are likely to be wrenched away from (films such as *Jaws* (1975) present this well, with the sense of normality contrasting with and heightening an oppressive feeling of impending danger). There is a third and less common way of introducing the protagonist and this is a slow build where they take time to emerge as the key character amongst an ensemble cast. This is difficult to write, and even harder to sell, despite its potential for success.

Ideally, by ten pages into the screenplay (the point readers decide to continue or quit) a reader should be able to identify the protagonist, what their goal is and what they plan to do to achieve it. If a screenwriter has not been able to deliver this, then they can expect a lot of rejection slips.

Setting the style and pace – Put crudely, it is easy to work out whether a screenplay is aiming to be an action blockbuster or a romantic comedy from the number of scenes on its first few pages. The more scenes the faster the pace (the more likely it is to star Vin Diesel), whereas the fewer scenes the more leisurely the pace (the more likely it is to star Tom Hanks). This convention should prove invaluable to the screenwriter as if you are looking to produce an action screenplay and you can see a leisurely pace developing then you know you need to re-write shorter scenes in to pick up the pace.

Introduce the theme of the story – A theme emerges in the opening and so a screenwriter should not consciously try to write it in (some very bad writing can be produced in this way). If you look at the opening of *Saving Private Ryan* (1998) the theme of the futility of war is soon apparent, and from the grueling opening sequence it continues to grow. It is not explicitly expressed by any character, but emerges from the action that is written in. There is a piece of screenwriting folklore that says that the theme always appears on page three of a screenplay, and thinking this through there

Saving Private Ryan

is probably some logic to it – if you have not managed to express a theme by three minutes in, it probably means that the opening needs a re-write.

The ending is, of course, of equal importance (perhaps more to the audience than the reader) and it too has a number of things to achieve in order to be seen as successful:

Resolving External Conflict – External conflict includes the difficulties in relationships expressed throughout the screenplay, difficulties with the physical environment, difficulties with authority, difficulties with forces (such as nature), etc. Part of the thrill of story is in the conflict a character faces, and the satisfaction in the ending comes not only in these conflicts being tied up and resolved, but also in the *way* they are tied up and resolved. Ideally the seeds for the ending are placed somewhere in the last act and so there is a logic and a linear development to how the end is reached, and this should support the ways in which resolution is achieved. Magic fairies waving their wands to resolve things are fine in pantomime, but in screenplays the reader feels cheated unless the resolution has a through line back into the rest of the story.

Resolving Internal Conflict – Internal conflict comes from the gap that opens between how a character sees themselves and what they want, and how they discover they really are and what it is they actually need. Closing this gap is how the screenwriter creates resolution, and the ending invariably links back to the opening reminding the audience of the journey the protagonist has taken and the character development that has occurred.

There are basically two types of ending that achieve these objectives to varying degrees. The first is the unambiguous ending that is structured around cause / effect and conflict / resolution. This is the primary form adopted by most mainstream commercially successful

Hollywood films. The second is the ambiguous ending which although may offer a concrete physical resolution it offers a much less clear resolution to internal conflict, and the screenplay provokes more questions than it does answers in relation to its theme. Here, whilst the ending may reflect the opening, it does not offer closure, instead using the lack of closure to take the story off the page, off the screen and away into the lives of the audience where it will be considered, discussed and interrogated. Both types are successful in affecting audience – you just have to choose what you want to achieve from the ending.

SPECIALIST SCREENPLAY OPPORTUNITIES

So far I have considered mainstream feature film and television drama as the focus for developing your skills as a screenwriter. However, these are but two of an ever-expanding range of markets for your talents, and it is vital that you have a basic understanding of the requirements of each form. This will enable you to work across fields and gain experience in short-form work before undertaking larger projects. The main areas for consideration are commercials, documentary, music promotional videos, the short film and television situation comedies.

Commercials: Since advertising using the moving image was originally cinema-based, it utilises the Master Scene Script format, and since many commercials still start their life as part of the movie package at a cinema, this remains an appropriate format. There are three essential ingredients to making a commercial screenplay work:

Expressing the message – All advertising has a core message that should be expressed about the product, a message that goes beyond the simple 'buy me'. There are no hard and fast rules here, but essential to success is an understanding of the defined target audience. Consider private health insurance: would you try to promote it in the same way to a 50-year-old, as you would a 20-year-old? I wouldn't. Indeed, for the 20-year-old I'd probably make it very little about health *per se* and much more about image.

Show the benefits – The adage 'don't tell, show' is even more important in commercials since an image of someone enjoying the benefits of a product far outweighs the effects of being told about the benefits. Adverts for chocolate seldom bother to tell you about the percentage of cocoa in the chocolate, but they do show people experiencing pleasure on eating some.

AIDA – This acronym stands for **Attention, Interest, Desire, Action**. The screenplay should grab the audience's attention immediately – there is no time for a slow burn in a 30-second commercial. With their attention grabbed it needs to be sustained through creating interest in the product – this is usually through images of the product being used. Interest needs to be converted to desire, most likely by getting them to identify with people (like them) who are seen enjoying the benefits of the product. The intention of the commercial is that the desire will provoke action, the adoption of the product. The end of the commercial should instruct the audience how they can adopt the product and should reinforce the benefits one last time to convince them.

Documentary: Documentary makers often decry producing a script before they shoot, claiming the construction is all in the edit. However, I believe that the documentary script becomes a two-stage working document, which begins life effectively as a list of intentions and then (prior to the edit once all the rushes have been logged) revised into a final script.

Although documentary began its life as a film product, it does not use a Master Scene Script format. Instead it uses a form of the two-column television script.

EXAMPLE TWO COLUMN DOCUMENTARY SCRIPT FORMAT

Lost Villages, Lost Lives	
Helicopter fly by of markings in fields of trackways and lost buildings	Title sequence Music
Fields Pond Ruined chapel Apple orchards Local vineyard Oast house in early morning mists	Intro 160 years ago at the bottom of the valley was a thriving community of over 200 families, all working the land. On an ancient tradeway between the two surviving villages of B... and W... Monks founded a monastery here over a 1000 years ago attracted by the hot springs. Apples and wine. Hops and Barley.
Photo of Agricultural Labourer Photo of Hop Pickers Photo of Harvest	Summary of the life of an agricultural labourer – the people who once lived in the village.
Presenter in field walking the faint marks of boundaries and buildings	Identifying the questions to answer. Who were these people? How did they live? What brought an end to the village? Where did the people go?
Interview with local historian	Summary of history of village
Interview with relative of 'lost' village resident	Introduction of relative with anecdote

Lost Villages, Lost Lives	
Archeologists digging site Map of site superimposed on site	Summary of finds, and of the information constructed about the site. Walk through the site identifying key features

The left-hand column deals with visual material, be it moving images, stills, computer generated imagery, etc., and simply lists them with little view of how they will be used. The right-hand column identifies the commentary aspects of the documentary and frames them as actions, statements and questions. These will guide the production process, not dictate it, allowing for the flexibility necessary in documentary making, and allowing the crew to adapt to the location and to the opportunities presented on the day.

Once the material is shot then this same script will be revised and will be fleshed out with detail. The left-hand column will offer precise step by step, shot by shot, visuals and the right-hand column will have the commentary script 'as read' matched to the image.

Music Promotional Videos: These are a relatively new form (purpose designed as promotional tools since the early 1980s, though existing as films prior to this) and accordingly they do not follow any particular established form. I have seen them use the Master Scene Script format and I have also seen them use the television two column script.

Most importantly in whichever format used is the attention to timing. Everything in the music promo should be based around the timing that comes from the music track, and its associated rhythms and parts. This has led to the emergence of a specific form based around the Master Scene Script:

Music Promotional Video Format

00:00 – 00:15

Out of the early morning mists the Lead Singer rides furiously towards a Tuscan hill town that is lit by the first rays of the dawn sun. Howling and slavering behind him appears a horde of vicious brigands, riding dark horses, with braying hounds running ahead and a troop of evil looking dark heavy wagons that crunch through the landscape, steamrollering all before them.

00:16 – 00:25

We focus in on a beautiful flaxen haired woman asleep in a four-poster bed in a minimalist hall-like bedroom. It is darkly lit with candles, though a few rays of sunlight are breaking through the shuttered windows. She stirs, then rises in the bed an anxious look falling across her face.

00:26 – 00:40

The Lead Singer rides the wind through the arched gateway to the town, waking the other Band Members as he passes. They watch him ride up a narrow cobbled street, then turn as one to see the brigands bearing down on them. Quickly they close the town gates and begin barricading them.

You'll note that once again, individual shots are not referred to (but are inferred) within the overall 'feel' of a scene. The scenes are defined by the timeline of the music track and are not identified by Slugline. This does not present too much of a difficulty as the Slugline information is built into the fabric of the description, and it will be transposed into a shooting script (where individual shots and shot durations are established) by the production company.

Short Film: By its nature as film this format uses the Master Scene Script format, but is structured radically differently due to the demands of the inherent time constraint ('short film' being defined as anything from 10–30 minutes in the UK and Europe and up to 45 minutes in the US). There is little scope for anything other than a minimalist plot and character sketching in the short, and the complexity of the characterisation and multiple plot layers of the feature have no relation to this form. The most common mistake in writing the short is to see it as related to the feature, either as a promo, a sequence from a feature or a cut-down version of a feature.

There are six common types of short film, each lending itself to a particular length and style:

The character in crisis – This usually suits the longer form as it follows a similar approach as the feature in presenting a character with a problem that they have to solve, and in the solving of it they learn something about themselves. This is hard to do in 30 minutes and near impossible to do in ten. Often tragedy, sometimes comedy based.

The ordeal – This centres on a character having to face someone or a situation and survive it. It can be as simple as a job interview, a blind date, or charting the labyrinth to meet the Minotaur.

The circular narrative – A character sets out on a task and follows a path that leads to eventual success. Despite this, however, they find themselves back where they started (this can be a negative circle or a positive circle, depending on where you want to leave the audience).

The jack in the box – This follows a predictably progressing situation that leads to a surprise ending. This is often suited to the shortest of the short film forms, and more often than not adopts a comedic approach. Certainly one of the most seen forms of short.

The journey – This follows the agony of decision or arrangement around a journey. It is a generally predictable form that ends at the point the protagonist starts off on the journey (or decides to do something else instead).

The twist in the tail – The most common of all short film forms in which the audience is led to believe one thing and another thing is revealed in the final moments instead. Successful because it is often short and sharp, and because it uses either shock or comedy to deliver the twist just before it ends.

Television situation comedy: This has been the Holy Grail of both British and American television for a number of years now, and in part is why BBC3 has developed in the way it has. In the past 'sitcom' allowed time to develop an audience, perhaps over a couple of series, whereas now, with television so ratings-driven, if a sitcom does not hook an audience within the first series (sometimes just the first three episodes) then it gets pulled. Worth noting that under these strictures the writers of *Dad's Army* (1968-1977), *The Good Life* (1975-1978), *One Foot in the Grave* (1990-2000), and even *Only Fools and Horses* would not have seen a second series deliver them a paycheck. It is not only in the UK that ratings and focus groups have become a feature of the screenwriter's landscape – the experience is similar if not heightened in America, and whilst *Frasier* (1993-2004) was a successful series in its own right, *Cheers* (1982-1993), the slow-burn series that spawned it would probably not survive past a first series in today's market.

A sitcom uses the standard television two-column script layout and in the UK it is usually between 22 and 28 minutes long (depending if it is for commercial television or the BBC), and divides into three-acts (Act One covers the first 6–7 pages, Act Two the

Only Fools and Horses

next 11–13 pages and Act Three the last 5–8 pages). The first act sets up the principal storyline, and alerts the audience to which of the characters will be this episode's focal point. Act Two is the longest and sometimes bridges the commercial break, if there is to be one. It is where the storyline is developed and where the problem or question posed by that storyline has a solution identified. Act Three is the shortest act and offers the resolution. The American model is different, revolving around the need for frequent ad breaks, and so a half hour sitcom can come in as short as 18-20 minutes, and is usually structured around five acts. This tends to mean that American series tend to be punchier and leaner, and a very different animal to the more leisurely UK sitcom.

Each act is broken down into scenes (the number of which depends on the style of sitcom – *Seinfeld* (1990-1998) has a slower pace and so has fewer scenes, whereas *Scrubs* (2001-) is faster paced and so has more scenes). The scenes are normally 'gag' based in UK comedy, and so can be broken down further into set-up and punchline, with one character delivering the set-up, the unfunny part of the joke or the 'straight' situation, that allows another character to deliver the punchline, the joke that rises out of the interplay with the situation. American sitcom tends to revolve more around the humour of situations and embarrassments, and around actions and misunderstandings, with snappy funny lines facilitating the 'joke' running across scenes or even across the whole episode. Being less tied to a 'gag count' and more in tune with a cumulative sense of the development of comedy has meant that American sitcom has taken the lead in terms of defining the genre.

There is a current trend towards the 'cold opening' (best demonstrated by *Friends*), which is a pre-credit scene that is there either to set up the episode's story or to present a 'funny' scene that has little relevance to the rest of the episode, but puts the audience in the right frame of mind to engage and appreciate the episode. After its successful deployment in numerous American sitcoms, it has become a fixture of recent British sitcoms, especially if they are trying to mark themselves out as 'young' and 'fresh'.

The 'sitcom' revolves around a 'situation' – usually a familiar environment such as home or the workplace, with an occasional excursion to other familiar environments such as the local bar. Within that situation are a group of familiar people who are the regular episode after episode cast. These characters become our friends, and we get to know the details of their lives through the situations they are placed in. The situations they find themselves in can usually best be described as an unfamiliar take on the familiar, and it is this that allows the audience to connect, whilst giving room for comedic potential. There is usually more than one storyline being carried (though only one will be the important one to the episode) and (depending on the intention behind the series as a whole) this may focus on a particular character or be seen from the point of view of a particular character. Thus in *Frasier* the majority of storylines focused on Dr Frasier Crane, though as the series progressed Martin, Niles, and Daphne all had storylines centred on them. There may be serial elements to a sitcom (elements of story that carry across episodes) and this is very much determined by the style and type of sitcom (fast paced tend to have less serial elements, whilst the slower paced series have the time to deal adequately with the serial elements without compromising storylines or for that matter comedy).

The key to good sitcom structure is in setting up questions at the start of each episode. These questions (will Ross make a play for Rachel?, Will Daphne discover Nile's secret?, etc.) drive the narrative along and produce opportunities for comedy and pleasure. They reach a head in the climax before being largely answered in the resolution. However if serial elements are a significant feature to the series structure then some of the questions will roll across episodes and in some cases across whole seasons.

You should by now have worked out that there are countless opportunities for placing screenplays in various sections of the industry, and that whilst they all differ (in some cases considerably) from each other there are a number of elements that are consistent in developing the screenplay, irrespective of its format or audience. These elements, as described in each chapter of this book, form the craft of screenwriting, the firm and solid structure on which imagination, art, and talent can build and flourish. A craft is practiced until knowledge and confidence firm it. Imagination, art, and talent are often left untapped for want of a solid support. By practicing the craft skills outlined here the screenplays you want to write will come. Through perseverence, your imagination, art and talent will flourish and you will write the screenplays you never knew were yours to write.

The cast of
Frasier

[1] Aristotle, *Poctics*, trans. John Warrington Dent, 1963

[2] Griffith, D., *A Crash Course in Screenwriting*, 2004, p.41

[3] Hague, M., *Screenplay Structure - The Five Key Turning points of All Successful Scripts*, Screenplay Mastery Newsletter, 2006 http://www.screenplaymastery.com/structure.htm

GLOSSARY OF SCREENWRITING TERMS

A

act: a section of a screenplay that is defined by what it achieves – set up, development, resolution, etc.

action description: the description of what is happening on screen, the things that are seen.

adapted screenplay: a screenplay based on an original source such as a book or a play.

antagonist: a character that creates barriers and reversals, whose aim is to prevent the protagonist's success.

antihero: a non-conventional protagonist, who may even be unlikable (at least at the start).

archetype: a universal character that is the root of many other characters.

atmosphere: the dominant emotional *feel* in a screenplay.

audio: sound – a useful narrative tool, and also a great tool for scene setting.

B

background: descriptive of anything happening behind the main, foregrounded action. Useful to consider the narrative planes a scene offers (while two people converse in the foreground, a truck can be being stolen in the background).

backstory: incidents from a character's past that are usually alluded to either to move the narrative forward, or to develop characterisation.

barrier: an obstacle placed in the way of a protagonist (often in the first and second acts).

beat: (1) a unit of action within a scene or act that marks the subtle change of plot direction; (2) a dialogue instruction that tells an actor to pause briefly (e.g. 'holds for a beat').

C

catalyst: a character, or event that drives the protagonist towards a course of action (usually towards achieving their goal).

cause-and-effect: a 'logical' sequence of events in which one action or event is the cause of subsequent actions or events.

character: a person (this may be an animal, a daemon, or a cartoon teapot) that populates the world of the screenplay.

character arc: the line of character development across the screenplay.

character development: the revelation of information about characters across the screenplay, that enables an audience to make sense of them. It can also enable the character to make sense of themselves.

characterisation: the constructional elements of visualising a character for the screen.

character profile: a written description of a character's internal and external characteristics that enables the creation of 'realistic' characters.

cliché: an overused setting, piece of action, or lines of dialogue.

climax: the highpoint of a screenplay where all the main storylines come together and where usually the protagonist faces a win or lose point. The climax comes just before the resolution.

complication: an action or event that is placed early in a screenplay seemingly to little significance. It later is recognised as of key significance to the protagonist achieving their goal.

composite character: a character that is created from the combination of two or more characters that are compressed into one for structural or narrative reasons.

conflict: the key to any story. Internal or external opposition between a character and themselves / their situation / another character, a philosophy, or an event.

continuous: instead of placing DAY or NIGHT at the end of a Slugline, CONTINUOUS is placed to indicate that the action moves across locations with no timeline interruptions – particularly useful in chase sequences.

D

dénouement: the resolution of a plot.

development: (1) the period in which a screenplay is taken from draft to final draft under the guidance of a production company; (2) the period in which the screenplay is taken from script to screen (through production planning, budgeting, casting, scheduling, etc.).

dialogue: the words a character uses. When used well, it expresses both characterisation and subtext.

diegesis/diegetic: the world the characters live in (this includes the sights, sounds, etc.).

draft: a version of a screenplay. Screenplays will go through successive drafting in order to satisfy all those who become involved in getting it to screen.

E

exposition: the 'telling' of story in order to move the narrative forward. Too much exposition (particularly in dialogue) is the mark of a novice screenwriter.

EXT: abbreviation used in sluglines to define an exterior scene. Particularly useful in enabling the estimation of a screenplay's likely budget.

F

flashback: a scene that is the visualised memory of a character.

format: specified layout (including font, font size, and spacing) for a screenplay that is dependent on the exhibition medium. Not using the correct format when submitting an 'on-spec' screenplay is likely to result in it not even being looked at.

G

genre: a type of film with familiar codes and conventions, stories, plots, and themes.

I

idiot plant: a character, action, line of dialogue, etc., placed in a screenplay for the sole (and all too obvious) purpose of serving the plot.

INT: abbreviation used in sluglines to define an interior scene. Used in pre-production to calculate the cost of locations or set construction.

intercut between: right of page editing instruction that prepares the reader for a section of script with short scenes intercut with other short scenes. Usually an instruction 'END INTERCUTTING' will indicate the end of this section.

internal logic: somewhat illogical actions, events, settings, etc., that develop logicality within the world of the screenplay (a door in a wall can lead into John Malkovich's brain!!).

J

jeopardy: an action or event that makes the protagonist risk their goal.

L

linear structure: a chronological 'telling' of the narrative.

log line: a short, snappy description of the story used to define the story or 'pitch' the screenplay ('It's *Independence Day* meets *Only Fools and Horses*, the victory of the little man over the Universe').

M

MacGuffin: a plot device that seems to drive the narrative, and yet has little real significance in itself (Hitchcock famously used this as a technique – the robbery at the start of *Psycho* drove the narrative and yet had little relevance to the events other than inciting the characters on their journeys.)

mid-point realisation: a point (usually exactly in the middle of the screenplay) where the protagonist learns something about themselves – something that spurs them towards the resolution.

montage: sequenced images (sometimes very brief scenes) that compress time in order to offer exposition or character development.

motivation: the reason behind a character's actions or dialogue. The screenwriter should be prepared for the question 'What is the character's motivation here?'

mythic story: a story or part of a story (setting, action, character, etc.) that is a 'universal' appearing across time and across cultures.

N

narration: a disembodied voice (usually of a character from the diegetic world) that sets the scene for the story, links sections of story, or offers a conclusion to the story.

narrative: the part of the wider story chosen for inclusion in the screenplay.

non-diegetic: the world outside the character's world (this will include titles, theme music, etc.).

O

objective: the protagonist's key goal.

obstacle: a barrier placed in the way of a protagonist achieving their goal.

off-screen: descriptive of a character's off-screen voice, identified by O/S in parentheses after the character name.

omniscient narrative: a story told from a point of view that is not restricted to a single character.

original screenplay: a screenplay that has not been derived from another source.

P

pace: the rhythm and speed of story delivery across a script, that balances the demands of character development and plotting, with exposition.

page calculation: a page of script generally equates to a minute of screen time. Knowing this enables the calculation of budget, and ultimately of script viability.

parallel narrative / parallel action: having two things happening in separate places simultaneously.

parenthetical: the tone description (in parentheses under the character name) that points to the delivery of a line of dialogue (or a whole speech).

plant: the placing of information early in a screenplay that becomes significant at a later point.

pitch: the verbal 'selling' of a screenplay concept to a producer, company, or investor.

plot: the structuring of the narrative.

plot point: a moment in a screenplay (an action, a piece of dialogue, etc.) that spins the narrative off in a different direction. Plot points are usually the markers of a scene change.

point of view: a choice of perspective made by the screenwriter in constructing a scene. A scene will play differently depending on which character's point of view is adopted.

protagonist: the principal character whose actions move the narrative forward and whom the audience identifies or connects with.

R

red herring: a device that is used to point the audience in a 'wrong' direction, or to point them away from a solution in order to delay the resolution (see MacGuffin).

resolution: the final act of a screenplay where all (or most) of the storylines are resolved (unless setting up a sequel).

reversal: an obstacle (that generally comes towards the end of the second act) that sets the protagonist back in their efforts to achieve their goal.

S

scene: action and dialogue that is contained in one setting. It may spread across more than one interconnected location as long as the action or dialogue connects the locations (e.g. walking from an office, down a corridor, and into an atrium).

screenplay: the written description of a story specifically for the moving image.

setting: the diegetic place where a scene happens.

set-up: the opening act of a screenplay in which the audience is presented with the principal characters, information about the diegetic world, and the central premise of the story.

slug line: the scene heading offering information to set the scene (interior or exterior, location, day or night).

step outline: scene headings and one-line scene descriptors that are sequenced to make sense of the plotted story before the screenplay is written.

stereotype: an instantly recognisable character, location, action, etc. Negatively a stereotype implies overuse and lazy writing. Positively, it can be useful 'narrative shorthand' shared by the audience.

subplot: a secondary plot that has its own structure within the narrative and may intersect with the main plot at the climax.

subtext: the 'hidden' meaning / intentions of actions and dialogue.

synopsis: a succinct summary of the story as plotted, often used in 'selling' the screenplay.

T

theme: the 'message' of the screenplay.

three-act structure: beginning, middle, and end of a story, developed linearly (as defined by Aristotle).

transition: a right of page editing instruction that defines how one scene moves into the next. There is no need to offer such instructions for every scene, rather they should be presented in exceptional circumstances.

treatment: a detailed breakdown of the screenplay in prose form that offers a continuous step-by-step summary. A feature film treatment usually runs to between five and twenty-five pages.

U

unity: the interrelation of story components that combine to create a whole. The key to introducing and using components is to ensure that the unity of the screenplay is not compromised.

universals: characters, actions, dialogue, etc., that serve to represent something more than just their purpose in the diegetic world, something about what it is to be human.

V

version: a subjective flashback where a 'guess' is made to past events, or where the events are seen only from a partial point of view (made popular by the *CSI: Crime Scene Investigation* creators, and by Quentin Tarantino in *Pulp Fiction*).

visual: the elements in a screenplay that can be seen.

voiceover (V/O): disembodied dialogue or narration that is placed over visuals. This is a particularly powerful tool in documentary screenplays.

BIBLIOGRAPHY

Aristotle	*Poetics* trans John Warrington (Dent) 1963
Bell, J & Magrs, P.	*The Creative Writing Coursebook* (Macmillan) 2001
Blacker, I.	*The Elements of Screenwriting* (Macmillan) 1986
Blum, R.	*Television and Screen Writing: from Concept to Contract* (Focal) 1995
Brady, B & Lee, L.	*The Understructure of Writing for Film and Television* (University of Texas, Austin) 1988
Brady, J.	*The Craft of the Screenwriter* (Simon and Schuster, New York) 1981
Brande, D.	*Becoming a Writer* (Macmillan) 1996
Byrne, J.	*Writing Sitcoms* (A C Black) 2003
Cambell, J.	*The Hero With a Thousand Faces* (Fontana) 1993
Cooper, D.	*Writing Great Screenplays for Film and TV* (Macmillan, US) 1997
Cowgill L.J.	*Writing Short Films* (Lone Eagle) 1997
Dancyger, K.	*Broadcast Writing* (Focal) 1991
Dancyger, K. & Rush, J.	*Alternative Scriptwriting: Writing Beyond the Rules* (Focal) 1991
Dick, B.	*Anatomy of Film* (St. Martins Press) 3rd Ed. 1998
Dymtryk, E.	*On Screenwriting* (Focal) 1985
Elsey E. & Kelly A.	*In Short* (BFI) 2002
Field, S.	*Screenplay* (Dell) 1979
Field, S.	*The Screenwriter's Workbook* (Dell) 1982
Froug, W.	*Screenwriting Tricks of the Trade* (Silman-James, Beverly Hills) 1993
Gordic, V.	*Female Characters in Chaucer's 'Canterbury Tales' and Some Recent Approaches to the Theory of Character* at http://www.wgsact.net/e-library/elib0005.html
Griffith, D. A.	*A Crash Course in Screenwriting* (Scottish Screen) 2004
Grove, E.	*Raindance Writers' Lab: Write and Sell the Hot Screenplay* (Focal) 2001
Hague, M.	*Screenplay Structure: The Five Key Turning Points of All Successful Scripts* 2002 at www.screenplaymastery.com/structure.htm
Hatcher, J.	*The Art and Craft of Playwriting* (Story Press, Cincinnati) 1996
Hicks, N.	*Screenwriting 101* (Michael Wiese) 1999

Hoffman, A.	*Research for Writers* (Black) 1996
Howard, D. & Johnson C. H.	*Crafting Short Screenplays that Connect* (Focal) 2000
Mabley, E.	*The Tools of Screenwriting* (St Martins Press) 1993
Hunter, L.	*Screenwriting* (Hale) 1994
Lacey, N.	*Narrative and Genre* (Macmillan) 2000
Lee, R & Misorowski, R.	*Script Models* (Hastings) 1978
McKee, R.	*Story* (Methuen) 1998
Mehring, M.	*The Screenplay – A Blend of Film Form and Content* (Focal) 1989
Michaels, R.	*Megahit Movies* 1996 at www.megahitmovies.com/plotstry.htm
Miller, W.	*Screenwriting for Narrative Film and Television* (Columbus) 1988
Nash, C & Oakey, V.	*The Screenwriter's Handbook* (Harpers & Row) 1978
Owen, A. (ed.)	*Story and Character: Interviews with British Screenwriters* (Bloomsbury) 2003
Parker, P.	*The Art and Science of Screenwriting* (Intellect) 1998
Parker, P.	*Writing Short Films on ScreenOnline* 2004 at http://www.screenonline.org.uk/tours/shortfilm/tour1.html
Phillips, P.	*Understanding Film Texts* (bfi) 2000
Phillips W.H.	*Writing Short Scripts* (Syracuse University Press) 1991
Rabiger, M.	*Directing* (Focal) 1989
Rabiger, M.	*Directing the Documentary* (Focal) 1991
Rilla, Wolf.	*The Writer and the Screen* (W H Allen) 1973
Root, W.	*Writing the Script* (Henry Holt) 1979
Russell-Taylor, J.	*The Rise and Fall of the Well Made Play* (Methuen) 1967
Straczynski, J.	*The Complete Book of Scriptwriting* (Titan) 1997
Swain, D.	*Film Scriptwriting: A Practical Manual* (Focal) 2nd Ed. 1988
Upton, C. & Widdowson, J.	*An Atlas of English Dialects* (Oxford) 1996
Vale, E.	*The Technique of Screenplay Writing* (Souvenir) 1972
Vogler, C.	*The Writer's Journey* (Pan) 2nd Ed. 1998
Zaza, T.	*Script Planning* (Focal) 1993

INDEX

STILLS INFORMATION